BECOMING A CLINICAL PSYCHOLOGIST

Becoming a Clinical Psychologist: Everything You Need to Know brings together all the information you need to pursue a career in this competitive field.

This essential guide includes up-to-date information and guidance about a career in clinical psychology and gaining a place on clinical psychology training in the UK. It answers the questions all aspiring psychologists need to know, such as:

- What is clinical psychology?
- What is it like to train and work as a clinical psychologist?
- How do I make the most of my work and research experience?
- How do I prepare for clinical psychology applications and interviews?
- Is clinical psychology the right career for me?

By cutting through all the jargon and providing detailed interviews with trained and trainee clinical psychologists, *Becoming a Clinical Psychologist* will provide psychology graduates or undergrads considering a career in this area with all the tools they need.

Steven Thomas Mayers is a UK trained clinical psychologist currently working in Sydney, Australia. Since 2007, Steve has worked in a wide range of contexts with a variety of service user groups and professional teams in mental health, physical health, neuropsychology and social care settings in the UK and Australia.

Amanda Lindiwe Mwale is a Zimbabwe-born clinical psychologist who trained and currently works in London, UK. Amanda has worked in and conducted research with different groups of individuals and in a variety of clinical settings, including neuropsychology, developmental psychology, health psychology, adult mental health and intellectual disabilities.

BECOMING A CLINICAL PSYCHOLOGIST

EVERYTHING YOU NEED TO KNOW

steven thomas mayers and
amanda lindiwe mwale

LONDON AND NEW YORK

First published 2019
by Routledge
2 Park Square, Milton Park, Abingdon, Oxon OX14 4RN

and by Routledge
711 Third Avenue, New York, NY 10017

Routledge is an imprint of the Taylor & Francis Group, an informa business

British Library Cataloguing in Publication Data
A catalogue record for this book is available from the British Library

Library of Congress Cataloging in Publication Data
Names: Mayers, Steven Thomas, author. | Mwale, Amanda Lindiwe, author.
Title: Becoming a clinical psychologist : everything you need to know /
    Steven Thomas Mayers and Amanda Lindiwe Mwale.
Description: Abingdon, Oxon ; New York, NY : Routledge, 2018. | Includes
    bibliographical references.
Identifiers: LCCN 2018008059| ISBN 9781138223400 (hardback) |
    ISBN 9781138223417 (pbk.) | ISBN 9781315268453 (master) |
    ISBN 9781351976091 (web) | ISBN 9781351976084 (epub) | ISBN
    9781351976077 (mobipocket)
Subjects: | MESH: Psychology, Clinical | Career Choice
Classification: LCC RC467 | NLM WM 21 | DDC 616.89—dc23
LC record available at https://lccn.loc.gov/2018008059

ISBN: 978-1-138-22340-0 (hbk)
ISBN: 978-1-138-22341-7 (pbk)
ISBN: 978-1-315-26845-3 (ebk)

Typeset in Times New Roman
by Swales & Willis Ltd, Exeter, Devon, UK

CONTENTS

Acknowledgements   vi
How to use this book   vii
Key terms and organisations   x
Introduction   xiii

1   What is a clinical psychologist?   1
2   What is it like to train as a clinical psychologist?   22
3   What is it like to work as a clinical psychologist?   43
4   How can I make the most of my psychology degree and work experience?   65
5   How do I prepare for applications and interviews, and take care of myself?   90
6   How do I know if clinical psychology is for me?   111

Conclusion   133
Appendix: summary of charities for volunteer opportunities   136
References   139
Index   141

ACKNOWLEDGEMENTS

Steve would like to thank his parents, whose unconditional support has enabled him to make the most of a variety of opportunities. He would like to thank his friends, clients, supervisors and mentors in his career so far, who have supported him with this project and have contributed in a variety of ways.

Amanda would like to thank her family and for all their support and encouragement. A special thank you to her loving mother and brother, who are her biggest cheerleaders. She would also like to thank the people who have helped to put this book together including the editor, Joanne, who believed in this project and supported this book. She also thanks the amazing people who took their time out to proofread and add suggestions to make this work the best that it could be.

Both Steve and Amanda would both like to thank the trainee clinical and qualified clinical psychologists who took their time to complete the questionnaires and profiles. In particular, for sharing in the idea to bring their experience and knowledge together in this book; they couldn't have done this without them! They would also like to thank, Matthew Price and Sarah Spencer who edited the first version of the book and Lucy Johnstone and Imogen Rushworth who were kind enough to provide feedback and endorsement.

HOW TO USE THIS BOOK

This book is relevant to a wide range of people, including those considering studying clinical psychology and looking to apply to a clinical psychology training course in the future. We have highlighted some key section titles that occur regularly throughout the book which are designed to help you navigate your way through and engage with the content.

WHAT TRAINEE CLINICAL PSYCHOLOGISTS HAD TO SAY!

Whenever you see this title, the information that we present is from a survey we conducted online using a group of trainee clinical psychologists. In total 70 trainee clinical psychologists that were enrolled onto a doctoral programme responded to 20 questions about their pre-training and training experiences. The data gathered from these respondents are presented as either graphs or quotations. Where quotations are presented, we have organised them into broad themes to help make the information more accessible.

The trainee clinical psychologists who responded to the survey were mostly female (87%) and aged 25–32 (84%; 8% were under 24 and 8% were over 32). They had completed a range of higher education courses before training (all had an undergraduate degree, 58% had a Master's Degree, 4% had a PhD and 16% had a Postgraduate Diploma) and most had applied to training twice (56%; 12% applied once, 34% three times and 8% four times). The trainee clinical psychologists were from 12 UK doctorate courses (there are 30 courses in total), therefore their responses are not necessarily representative of all trainee clinical psychologists. Please bear this in mind when considering their experiences and advice.

HAVE A GO!

Whenever you see this title, there is an option to complete a practical task which will enable you to apply some of the information that you will have considered in the preceding section of the book. The 'Have a go!' section will invite you to think about your experiences and to write your ideas down. For example, in Chapter 5, 'How do I prepare for application and interviews, and take care of myself?', you have an opportunity to think about the reasons that you might want to be a clinical psychologist. The 'Have a go!' section in this chapter of the book looks like this:

Have a go!

- Write a list of reasons why you want to be a clinical psychologist.
- Write down your thoughts about what you would bring as a clinical psychologist that is unique.
- Write how your personal journey has led you to this career.

These sections of the book are optional but may help you to engage more with the content.

PROFESSIONAL PROFILES

To give you a detailed understanding of what it is like to train and work as a clinical psychologist, we created a more detailed interview which was completed by six trainees and six qualified clinical psychologists. These are presented as 'profiles' in Chapters 2 and 3: 'What is it like to train as a clinical psychologist?' and 'What is it like to work as a clinical psychologist?' The respondents gave detailed responses to a range of questions, describing where they work, how they have found training/qualified life, why they chose to train as a clinical psychologist, their experience of diversity in the profession, advice for an aspiring clinical psychologist and their interests outside of clinical psychology.

The demographic information for the respondents is provided with the profile. We asked trainee clinical psychologists from years one to three of the doctorate in clinical psychology to complete the profiles. The qualified clinical psychologists were selected to represent a range of services that a clinical psychologist might work within. The clinical psychologists we approached work in the following specialities: Forensic Services, Paediatric Health Psychology, Adult Mental Health Inpatient and Outpatient Services, Neuropsychological Rehabilitation and Adult Learning Disabilities Services. As we discuss in Chapter 1, 'What is a clinical psychologist?', there are a wide range of roles that a clinical psychologist can occupy. There is not scope within this book to present profiles for clinical psychologists working in every available service type and as with the trainee clinical psychologists, the responses are not necessarily representative of all clinical psychologists. Please bear this in mind when considering their experiences and advice.

SUMMARY

At the end of each chapter of the book we have provided a summary to make the information easier to digest, focusing on a few key points.

KEY TERMS AND ORGANISATIONS

As with most professions, clinical psychology is full of abbreviations which become routine for those within the profession and often serve to confuse those who are not! There are also sometimes different words for the same things. For example, people who are accessing services will often be referred to as 'service users', 'clients' or 'patients', depending on the type of service and the individual's preferred term. We have summarised the key terms and organisations that are useful for you to know before we explain more about how clinical psychologists work and who with.

Doctorate in Clinical Psychology (DClinPsy/DClinPsych/ ClinPsyD): this is the course that is completed by all clinical psychologists in the UK.

Why is it important? Some titles such as 'psychologist' are not protected in law. This means that one can call oneself a 'psychologist' without any specific qualifications and registration. However, you need to undertake the Doctorate in Clinical Psychology to legally be referred to as a 'clinical psychologist'. Interestingly, not all clinical psychologists will have a doctorate if they trained when the clinical psychology training course was a Master's level qualification or if they gained their qualification in some other countries.

Clearing House for Postgraduate Courses in Clinical Psychology: the 'Clearing House' is a non-profit educational charity that works with clinical psychology courses to provide information and facilitate the application process.

Why is it important? You use this website to obtain up to date information about current clinical psychology training courses and the application process. The Clearing House website is also used to submit any applications to train as a clinical psychologist.

The British Psychological Society (BPS): the British Psychological Society is a representative body for psychologists and psychology in the United Kingdom.

Why is it important? Clinical psychologists were required to register with the BPS until 1st July 2009 and they have been the traditional representatives of all psychology professions located in the UK.

The Division of Clinical Psychology (DCP): the DCP is a sub-group of the BPS which exists to promote the professional interests of clinical psychologists in the UK.

Why is it important? The DCP and BPS and have an important role in the development and representation of clinical psychology in the UK. A number of clinical psychologists are members of the BPS and DCP.

Association for Clinical Psychologists (ACP-UK): a collective of professionals working in clinical psychology felt that the DCP was not able to represent the profession adequately due to restrictions imposed by the BPS. In 2017, these professionals created a separate organisation to support clinical psychologists in a politically responsive way and work alongside the BPS and DCP.

Why is it important? This new organisation will be developing its role, identity and aims to represent clinical psychology in a responsive and politically active way.

Health and Care Professions Council (HCPC): the organisation that regulates the practice of clinical psychologists, and a wide range of other health professions, in the UK.

Why is it important? You are required to be registered with the HCPC in order to practice as a clinical psychologist.

Psychologists for Social Change (PSC): previously known as Psychologists Against Austerity, PSC is a network of applied psychologists, academics, therapists, psychology graduates and others who are interested in applying psychology to policy and political action. This organisation believes that people's social, political and material contexts are central to their experiences as individuals.

Why is it important? Clinical psychologists are increasingly involved in facilitating change beyond their usual ways of working. PSC are a good organisation to learn about if you're interested in these approaches.

INTRODUCTION

In June 2013, Steve and Amanda were two aspiring clinical psychologists who had recently secured a place on a clinical psychology training course after numerous unsuccessful attempts. They both felt fortunate to have the opportunity to train as clinical psychologists and grateful for the support they had on their journey to training. Between them, they had applied to training six times, had four interviews for training places and even more 'rejections'. On top of this, they had countless colleagues and friends who had been through this process alongside them and they felt very privileged to be part of a large, supportive and informative network. Steve and Amanda were aware that this wasn't the case for all people considering the profession of clinical psychology. As a result, they thought that sharing a wide range of experiences with those considering a career in clinical psychology would be valuable. They decided to bring this information together so that people who were interested in becoming a clinical psychologist could access it easily.

Steve and Amanda started working on the book as they began their clinical training in 2013 and are now both qualified clinical psychologists. Over the past four years, they have conducted surveys, interviewed trainee and clinical psychologists, spoken to friends, reflected on their own experiences, read articles and asked people considering the profession what they would like to know more about. What they've produced in this book is the result of that process. *Becoming a Clinical Psychologist: Everything You Need to Know* is your guide to clinical psychology as a profession and aims to help you decide if it is the career for you. If you are a Psychology A-level student, undergraduate, parent, careers advisor or a person about to undertake an interview for the training course, this book is for you. Steve and

Amanda hope you find the information useful and wish you well on your journey towards becoming a clinical psychologist!

The book is separated into six chapters, which will answer a range of relevant questions that someone considering a career in clinical psychology might ask such as, 'How do I make the most of my experience?' to 'How do I know if clinical psychology is for me?' Chapter 1 begins with an overview of what a clinical psychologist is, some reasons why people choose to become a clinical psychologist and how you can train as a clinical psychologist. In Chapter 2, a selection of six 'profiles' will be presented which give the reader an insight into the diverse range of experiences of people who are training as clinical psychologists. In Chapter 3, a selection of six 'profiles' will be presented for qualified clinical psychologists. These present the diverse experiences of people who are working, post-qualification, as clinical psychologists. Chapter 4 is for people who are considering studying psychology, undergraduates and those who have completed the relevant psychology degree and are ready for the next step. This section contains a summary of things to consider before and during the degree, what might be considered as relevant experience and how you can make the most of it. In Chapter 5, there is a summary of the advice that people have for anyone completing an application and preparing for interviews. This includes information about what the courses might want and how you can match your skills and values to a particular course. Being unsuccessful in the applications for training courses is very common and in Chapter 6 the focus shifts to how we can manage rejection and how this process provides a unique opportunity to consider your values and career choices.

Steve and Amanda hope that the information provided helps you in your consideration, decision making and preparation for becoming a clinical psychologist!

WHAT IS A CLINICAL PSYCHOLOGIST?

Clinical psychology can be described as the 'psychological specialty that provides continuing and comprehensive mental and behavioural health care for individuals and families; consultation to agencies and communities; training, education and supervision; and research-based practice' (APA, 2017). As this definition suggests, the role of a clinical psychologist is varied and continually changing in the context of Health and Social Care in the United Kingdom (UK). Clinical psychology did not always look like it does today, the profession is relatively young and has changed a great deal over the past 60 years. For an extensive understanding of the history and development of clinical psychology in the UK, see Hall, Pilgrim and Turpin (2015). Today, clinical psychologists generally work in Health and Social Care settings that include hospitals, health centres, Community Teams, Specialist Services and Social Services. Typically, they work as part of a larger team with other health professionals. Most of the clinical psychologists in the UK are employed by the National Health Service (NHS), some work for third sector organisations (such as charities), in private practices and some are engaged in community-based projects.

WHO DO CLINICAL PSYCHOLOGISTS WORK WITH?

Clinical psychologists are trained to work with people of all ages and often support some of the most vulnerable people in our society, which can include children adolescents, adults, couples, families and older adults. The support of these people

1

will usually take place in an Inpatient or hospital setting, or in Outpatient Services such as a clinic or in the community. Clinical psychologists work in Mental Health, Physical Health and other settings such as Learning Disabilities Services, Forensic Hospitals, Addiction Services, Brain Injury Rehabilitation Services, Homelessness Services, and others.

HOW DO CLINICAL PSYCHOLOGISTS WORK?

Many clinical psychologists work with people who are experiencing psychological distress. Examples of common difficulties that clinical psychologists come across are often described as depression, anxiety, psychosis, post-traumatic stress, addiction and so on. In the context of the common language used to categorise problems, clinical psychologists are less interested in how to label a problem but are more concerned with how to understand and make sense of it (Johnstone, 2000). Clinical psychologists would usually do four things when working with someone:

1   complete an assessment;
2   use the assessment to understand the client's difficulties (known as a formulation);
3   complete a therapeutic intervention;
4   evaluate the effectiveness of their approach.

Clinical psychologists are both 'scientist practitioners' and 'reflective practitioners' (Llewelyn & Murphy, 2014). As 'scientist practitioners', clinical psychologists use therapy approaches that research suggests are useful in helping people who are experiencing psychological distress. In addition, they can apply their understanding of psychological research and knowledge in different situations in a variety of ways. As 'reflective practitioners', clinical psychologists are encouraged to think about their work so that they can adapt to best support the individuals that they're working with. These approaches are emphasised throughout the training process with continued supervision and professional development.

Assessment

Clinical psychologists try to make sense of people's difficulties by gathering information (an assessment) and then trying to make sense of how the problem functions in that person's life (a formulation). The assessment process often considers a person's early life history, family history, including the quality of parenting, social history, close relationships, experiences of traumatic events, disadvantage, deprivation, disability and discrimination. The assessment will, whenever possible, be collaborative and involve the individual receiving psychological support. Often psychologists use an interview format to gather information, as well as using questionnaires to determine the severity of specific problems, e.g. sleep, low mood and anxiety. Sometimes clinical psychologists will need to carry out detailed specialised neuropsychological assessments, which assess the impact of conditions affecting the brain, such as brain injury, stroke and dementia. These are often carried out if a person experiences difficulty with their memory, information processing and attention span, amongst other things, which may be impacting on their wellbeing and quality of life. Psychologists can also gather information through observing behaviour, e.g. observing a child's classroom behaviour in a school for pupils with additional needs, making use of reports and information gathered by other professionals and relatives of individuals who require support.

Formulation

People who are experiencing psychological distress are often experiencing an understandable reaction to unusual or overwhelming events (Bentall, 2003). Whilst gathering information during the initial assessment, the clinical psychologist will work with the individual or team to develop a shared psychological understanding of the difficulties before determining what might be the most useful approach to supporting the person. As a result, it is important to consider the individual's background and life circumstances and how these experiences have impacted on their current problems. The formulation will attempt to make sense of the information gathered in the assessment and will also include information about factors which may keep the problem going and the things that might help to keep the person well. The psychological formulation can take various forms depending on the approach that the psychologist prefers to use. For a summary of the process and different types of formulation commonly used by clinical psychologists, see Johnstone and Dallos (2013).

Psychological intervention

Following assessment and formulation, psychological support will then be given to people who require it, sometimes using a specific form of psychotherapy. There are wide range of therapies, which you don't need to understand at this point, but they include Cognitive Behaviour Therapy (CBT), Compassion Focused Therapy (CFT), Acceptance and Commitment Therapy (ACT), Cognitive Analytic Therapy (CAT), Mindfulness Based Cognitive Therapy (MBCT), Dialectical Behaviour Therapy (DBT), Psychodynamic Psychotherapy (short- and long-term) and Systemic Family Therapy. Some clinical psychologists integrate elements of different models into their intervention to facilitate an individualised approach to therapy. Clinical psychologists can also facilitate group therapy sessions based on these models and those specific to group therapy, supporting people to develop coping skills for managing particular problems within a supportive and safe environment.

Evaluation

Before, during and after an intervention, clinical psychologists will be looking to evaluate their work. For example, if delivering therapy, the clinical psychologist may want the person receiving support to complete a questionnaire that provides a measure of a specific area of functioning, e.g. anxiety, as mentioned earlier, and they will want to determine if this has changed following the therapy. To do this, they will complete these measures again during and after therapy and then after several weeks following the intervention if possible.

The reason for doing this is to determine if the therapy has been useful for the person. Clinical psychologists will often use session-based measures to facilitate a conversation with the person receiving therapy about how they feel it is going and to make any adjustments if necessary.

Communication

Effective communication is central to the role of a clinical psychologist (Llewelyn & Murphy, 2014). Clinical psychologists are generally very good communicators with excellent literacy skills. Clinical psychologists will write reports to a wide range of people, including professionals and family members and they are able to adjust their face-to-face communication style to meet the needs of an individual. These skills in communication enable the clinical psychologist to be effective in a range of roles explored below.

Teaching and consultation

Clinical psychologists are often involved in the teaching via staff training to help improve interactions with service users that professionals may find challenging. This will usually be presented in a more structured way and could include training designed to equip nurses on a stroke and brain injury rehabilitation ward with skills in developing a behaviour support plan for a service user. Another example of a teaching role is providing individual or group supervision to trainee clinical psychologists or staff who are using psychological therapy. Consultation can involve developing psychological formulation and recommendations with other colleagues in both formal and informal ways. The consultation is often less structured than teaching and allows for staff members to have a conversation about concerns they may have from a psychological perspective. The consultation and teaching helps others to develop a psychologically informed understanding of teams, systems and an individual's difficulties, which they may find challenging.

Leadership and service development

The ability to communicate effectively and develop relationships with others is required for effective leadership and management. Clinical psychologists are particularly good at this because they have excellent communication skills and are trained to understand the human mind and behaviour. Relationships are fundamental to the practice of clinical psychology and are another aspect of what makes clinical psychologists excellent leaders. Clinical psychologists can also become leaders in the 'co-production' of services. This is due to their work experience and training in considering multiple perspectives of a problem, developing hypotheses and new ways to reconsider problems. They are also skilled in facilitating the participation of service users in the design and improvement of Health and Social Care Services that they use.

Wider systemic work

Some psychologists work in other ways, where they might focus on the causes of distress as a problem that exists within the wider 'systems' that surround a person, such as a family or community. When this is the case, the psychologist will usually apply the same approach of developing a formulation considering these wider systems. These psychologists sometimes work therapeutically with couples, families or a combination of staff and non-professionals. Systemic work encourages the inclusion of different perspectives, where the clinical psychologist avoids positioning themselves as an 'expert' who has all the necessary solutions and techniques. Instead, a clinical psychologist working in this way understands their role as facilitating people's use of their existing strengths and resources.

Other ways of working systemically include working more as a community psychologist. These psychologists are dedicated to developing ways of integrating psychological thinking within a community space rather than in conventional clinical settings. A central part of Community Psychology practice is focussing on social change necessary for the psychological wellbeing of disadvantaged communities, organisations and wider society.

If you are interested in the above then you can read online about 'Systemic Family Therapy', 'Community Psychology' and organisations like Psychologists for Social Change (McGrath, Walker & Jones, 2016).

Research

Clinical psychologists complete a doctorate level qualification which involves completing a novel piece of research over the three years of training. This is often in the format of a larger thesis, similar to a PhD or a number of smaller documents which can be published with less editing. This can be a very challenging part of the training, but it equips clinical psychologists with excellent research skills and the ability to facilitate future research and audit, using a variety of approaches. Clinical psychologists are also in a strong position to share high quality information about treatment effectiveness and Health Service performance to other clinicians or service commissioners. Clinical psychologists may work in research departments at universities and are mainly focused on academic work to advance future clinical practice. These clinical psychologists will sometimes continue to work in a clinical service at the same time.

Summary of roles

Overall, clinical psychologists can use their skills to work in a wide range of roles. As a result, their diverse clinical, research and leadership skills make them highly valuable members of Health and Social Care Teams across a wide range of services. Often, the work of a clinical psychologist has benefits for the broad spectrum of service 'stakeholders' who include people using services, their family, partners and the wider community.

UNDERSTANDING THE ROLE OF A CLINICAL PSYCHOLOGIST: MYTH BUSTING

There are several common associations with the term 'psychologist' and these misconceptions also relate to clinical psychology. For many people, the specific function of a clinical psychologist generally seems unclear amongst the slang, jargon and stereotypes, i.e. a Freud-like eccentric bearded man sat next to a person lying on a couch. To help provide some clarification on what a clinical psychologist is, it is useful to first bust some of the common myths!

Myth one: 'clinical psychologists are the same as psychiatrists'

When someone asks how psychiatrists and clinical psychologists differ, a clinical psychologist would usually explain that they do not need the medical training that a psychiatrist would require to practice. Rather, clinical psychologists receive specialist training in psychological theory, research and clinical practice, which includes psychotherapy skills. This training equips the clinical psychologist with the ability to understand and hopefully reduce psychological distress and improve wellbeing by developing a formulation of a person's difficulties in the context of their life experiences. Fundamentally, psychiatrists often consider the primary cause and method of treatment for psychological distress as biological, involving the brain, whereas clinical psychologists emphasise the importance of psychological and social factors. These factors may include a person's history and experiences, their relationships and their thoughts and behaviours. Clinical psychologists support an understanding of how these factors can be understood in order to support someone who is distressed. Psychiatrists generally prescribe medication and monitor its effects on the person's experience, whilst a clinical psychologist often offers talking therapy to support a person to understand their distress and develop ways to manage it. It is important to note that clinical psychologists' and psychiatrists' work is not always mutually exclusive. Both professions often work together to support a person using a combination of biological, psychological and social (known as bio-psycho-social) approaches to Mental Health Care.

Myth two: 'a clinical psychologist will try to "analyse" me'

The idea of analysis and psychology emerged as a result of Sigmund Freud's approach to working with people who are distressed.

This approach, called Psychoanalysis, is a type of therapy that focuses on our unconscious mind, amongst other things. Freud influenced our understanding of how the mind works and gave us many helpful ideas such as the unconscious mind, which is the part of our mind that we are unable to access with our thoughts. However, in psychoanalytic practice, the 'analysis' only happens in therapy when a person has consented to this process. Modern clinical psychology emphasises collaborative ways of understanding psychological distress. It focuses on enabling the person who is suffering to improve their awareness of what has happened to them and to consider what steps they can take in therapy and in other areas of their life to help improve their wellbeing.

Myth three: 'a clinical psychologist will try to read my mind'

Psychological magicians such as Derren Brown use psychological theory of behaviour to anticipate a person's response, and even though it may look like they're reading a participant's mind, they aren't. It's not possible to read another person's mind, though we can sometimes make an educated guess about how they may be feeling or what they may be thinking. We can do this by empathising with the person and considering how we might feel in the same situation. Clinical psychologists would work openly and aim to share understanding to avoid second-guessing another person's experience. This approach applies to their clinical work, where it is often seen unhelpful to take an 'expert position' when working with an individual or team as it is more important to enable the person to understand their own experiences and 'mind'.

Myth four: 'it's all a load of made-up mumbo-jumbo'

Our mind is complex and difficult to understand. Most people feel that they know themselves well and perhaps worry that someone else will try to understand them or that a secret might become known. When this happens, people may be sceptical about clinical psychology and suggest that it is unscientific. This isn't true as psychology is the scientific study of the human mind and behaviour. Clinical psychology involves applying well tested theory and evidence-based research to work with individuals and systems in distress – this is the 'scientist practitioner' role that was described above. There are different ways of responding to distress and some may appear different to others, but a clinical psychologist makes a decision based on theory or research evidence, rather than just making it up as they go along.

In summary, clinical psychologists are somewhat unique in how they help people who are distressed, they use the latest scientific research in their work and they won't try to analyse you or read your mind!

WHAT ARE THE CURRENT CHALLENGES FOR CLINICAL PSYCHOLOGISTS?

Clinical psychologists are a relatively small professional group and sometimes represent the minority of staff in a team and there are approximately only 12,000 clinical psychologists registered with the HCPC in the UK (Farndon, 2016), which is small in relation to other professions, i.e. there are 236,836 registered doctors in the UK (GMC, 2017). As a result, it can sometimes be challenging for the clinical psychologist's message to be heard and clinical psychologists have to work with and through other people. To do this, clinical psychologists often work with all aspects of the Health and Social Care system including people who are interested in psychological ideas and those who have authority to effect change (Georgiadis & Phillmore, 1985). There is a dominant emphasis on the 'medical model' of distress in Health settings and as discussed above in 'myth one', clinical psychologists work in different ways to psychiatrists. Therefore, other clinicians can have a vested interest in the medical approach and may find it challenging to incorporate alternative ways of understanding distress. This medical approach means that we often talk about distress as an 'illness' that requires 'treatment', which can be why we often hear these words when people talk about distress in the media. These ideas can sometimes make it hard for people to engage with psychological support that requires some self-management or when considering the multiple factors that can cause a person to feel distressed.

Government imposed austerity (often described as 'money saving') measures have meant that Health and Social Care Services have had to make cuts every year since 2010. As a result, this has increased pressures of services in which psychologists work and there has been a particularly large impact on Mental Health provision (McGrath, Walker & Jones, 2016). There is an emphasis on delivering therapy following a manualised approach (e.g. CBT) in order to increase the amount of people receiving support and improve waiting times. Some people suggest that these approaches are not as effective as they do not require highly specialist training and undervalue the relationship between the therapist and the client (Strupp & Anderson, 1997). Other professionals have some of the skills that clinical psychologists also have and are increasingly able to develop skills in delivering models of therapy, which means clinical psychology can be viewed as an expensive resource. Nevertheless, clinical psychologists are trained in multiple ways of managing distress and can work with a number of theories and ideas to consider the best way to support an individual or team. As considered above, they are also trained and skilled to work as teachers, consultants, researchers, can provide leadership to other professionals and work with the wider systems surrounding a person. Therefore, it is important that clinical psychology remains a valued resource across Social and Health Care Teams and departments.

WHY DO SOME PEOPLE WANT TO BECOME CLINICAL PSYCHOLOGISTS?

There are many factors that lead a person to decide to train as a clinical psychologist; this can include a mix of personal and professional experiences and a wide range of interests. Having a good sense of why they want to train as a clinical psychologist can help people through the more challenging parts of the application and training process.

What trainee clinical psychologists had to say!

To find out more information about why people choose to train as a clinical psychologist, we asked 70 trainee clinical psychologists from 12 training courses in the UK to answer the question: 'What drew you to a career in clinical psychology?' This question gave us more insight into some of the factors that encourage people to consider pursuing the career. The responses related to key themes: 'interested in the human experience', 'understanding personal challenges', 'a rewarding career', 'varied ways of working' and 'helping people who are distressed'.

Interested in human experience

Some trainee clinical psychologists were particularly drawn to the career because they were curious about learning more about the human mind and behaviour and what happens when someone is distressed.

> *'I have always had an interest and curiosity about people. . . and what makes us tick.'*

> *'An interest in human behaviour and fascination with people who are distressed.'*

> *'I've always been interested in psychology in terms of what motivates us as human beings, how we manage our relationships, personal, professional challenges and so on.'*

> *'I worked in the judicial system and was intrigued by the various stresses in people's lives and how they managed. I've always been fascinated by the way society views mental illness.'*

> *'An interest in the way the mind works and how we understand the world, combined with personal experiences of mental illness and an interest in helping others.'*

> *'I always questioned why people I knew acted in certain ways, why they were anxious and depressed. It was only when I started to study psychology that I realised that I could answer some, if not all, of these questions.'*

'An interest in eccentric people combined with a disinterest in the medical model. Therefore, being a mental health nurse or psychiatrist was not appealing to me.'

'I learnt about clinical psychology during my undergrad degree and it fascinated me.'

Understanding personal challenges

For some trainee clinical psychologists, one of the main drivers for their interest in the profession included their own personal experiences of difficulties. These include mental health problems and social inequalities that had an impact on their lives. The difficulties faced appeared to motivate these trainee clinical psychologists to pursue a career that would help them to develop their understanding of psychological problems and distress.

'What drew me to this career was my personal experience of mental health problems. I was also interested in what makes people behave and think the way they do.'

'When I was doing my A-levels, I chose psychology as an option in an attempt to help me understand more about mental illness because of my own experiences of mental illness in my immediate and wider family.'

'Members of my family had mental health problems and being part of their struggle drew me to a career in clinical psychology.'

'Experiencing prejudice from others towards me enabled me to understand what inequalities and discrimination feel like and knowing how this can affect individuals.'

'Whilst doing my degree a number of people close to me disclosed mental health problems they'd been struggling with which made me see the important contribution psychologists can give.'

'I had a personal experience with a clinical psychologist when I was 15 and it was not a good experience. This led me to look into the career and find out what it was meant to be about.'

A rewarding career

Through our research, it became clear that the potential to help others and contribute to their wellbeing was an important factor for the trainee clinical psychologists interviewed. Those who had explored other career options spoke about how they had been persuaded by what clinical psychology had to offer, in comparison to other professions.

> *'Wanting to help people. Not wanting an office job.'*

> *'My first degree was in graphic design. During my degree, I was chosen to work on a summer camp for children with learning disabilities and autism. Following this I became interested in understanding the children I had worked with and how I might help them and their families in the long-term. The experience inspired me to apply for a psychology conversion course.'*

> *'I did three weeks work experience with a clinical child psychologist and loved it. From then on, I knew that it was what I wanted to do.'*

> *'I wanted to do something that is useful to society in general.'*

> *'I was drawn to the range of skills gained through training and the broad spectrum of work that CPs do beyond just being a therapist.'*

> *'I like the fact that psychology draws upon numerous theories to contribute to understand somebody's difficulties.'*

> *'Aged 13, I asked my career advisor what the difference between a psychologist and a psychiatrist was, and they said a psychiatrist gives injections. I'm scared of needles, so I decided to become a psychologist!'*

Varied ways of working

Clinical psychologists can work in Clinical Services and in Research settings. When they work in Clinical Services, they are applying the research evidence to their every-day practice. This was appealing to some of the trainee clinical psychologists.

'Interesting, scientific, yet helping profession. Varied and have a chance to work in a variety of ways.'

'I came from a (none-applied) research background and I felt that this lacked in direct impact. I wanted to work with people and help them now, rather than in an indefinite amount of years.'

'Wanted a job combining academic and clinical aspects.'

Helping people who are distressed

The trainee clinical psychologists were motivated to pursue a career as a clinical psychologist because there was opportunity to support others and to help them to make changes in their lives.

'Having skills to help people in distress.'

'Supporting the individual to make a positive change in their lives.'

'The idea of using therapy skills to take a person through a journey of difficulty and helping them find the incredible light at the end of a dark and horrible tunnel is awesome.'

'I think that clinical psychologists are well placed in the NHS to influence change, particularly within Multi-Disciplinary Teams.'

'Wanting to work with people and an interest in studying since A-level.'

'My grandmother was a mental health nurse . . . wanting to work in a helping profession.'

'I always wanted to study medicine and had experience working in an oncology unit. During my time there, I was surprised by the psychological support for people newly diagnosed with cancer and seeing their reactions when being told they had cancer. It made me want to help, support and just be there for them during a difficult life event.'

'Understanding behaviour and supporting an individual to make a positive change in their lives.'

In summary, there are a variety of reasons why individuals might be drawn to a career in clinical psychology. These can arise from challenging personal experiences as well as a desire to learn more about psychology and to contribute to another person's wellbeing. The above responses might help you to consider the particular things that may appeal to you about this career. The process of figuring this out doesn't have to happen in an instant and reasons for wanting to pursue the career may change over time.

HOW TO BECOME A CLINICAL PSYCHOLOGIST IN THE UK

In order to become a qualified clinical psychologist in the UK, you will need to complete a three year, full-time, funded doctoral programme at one of the 30 universities that offer the training course. The course requires trainee clinical psychologists to complete four to six clinical placements, assessed academic work (usually exam and/or essay based) and a thesis which describes a unique piece of research undertaken by the trainee clinical psychologist. However, before you apply for a place on the doctoral training course, you will need to have the following:

A 2:1 (preferably a high 2:1 of around 67/100 or above) or first class undergraduate degree in psychology that is accredited by the British Psychological Society (BPS). If you don't have this, you might require further study, such as a Master's Degree or PhD, to show that you will be able to meet the academic demands of the course. If you already have an undergraduate degree in a different subject, you can complete a BPS approved postgraduate qualification or conversion course. More information regarding BPS accredited courses is available on their website (www.bps.org.uk/bpslegacy/ac). For international applicants, it is possible to apply for training in the UK providing that the pre-training qualifications and experience are equivalent to those obtained through study at UK universities. For more information about this, you can contact the Clearing House directly (www.leeds.ac.uk/chpccp).

In addition to the academic requirement, you are usually required to have completed at least one year or more of relevant clinical experience and/or research experience. A range of areas that one can obtain pre-training clinical experience are considered in Chapter 4, 'How can I make the most of my psychology degree and work experience?' Generally, successful applicants will undertake work or research posts for two to four years, or complete research, before gaining a place on the Doctorate in Clinical Psychology. This is because the doctorate is amongst the most popular postgraduate courses in the UK due to the fact it offers training in a range of approaches, which can be applied to a large number of settings. In addition to this, the training course is also currently funded, so the journey to obtain a place can be highly competitive.

Exceptions to the rule

The universities of York and Hull offer an undergraduate psychology degree which is directly linked to the University of Hull Doctorate in Clinical Psychology. Only undergraduates who study at Hull and York are eligible to apply to the University of Hull Doctorate in Clinical Psychology. If successful in their applications, these trainee clinical psychologists can either begin the Doctorate immediately after completing their undergraduate degree, or after one year of work experience. If you are interested in this route to clinical training, you can contact the training course at the University of Hull or either of the undergraduate psychology programs, at Hull and York universities, directly.

There are three UK courses which are offering self-funded places, and two of these will accept direct applications. These are much more expensive than the cost of an undergraduate degree and the competition for these places may vary and you can contact these courses directly for more information. The Clearing House website will have information about courses offering self-funded places in any given year.

Applying to train as a clinical psychologist in the UK

Once you have the relevant pre-training qualifications, research and/or work experience and feel ready to apply to train as a clinical psychologist, you should apply to train at the BPS approved Doctorate in Clinical Psychology via the Clearing House for

Postgraduate Training Courses website. Information about all courses can be found at www.leeds.ac.uk/chpccp/index.html or by searching for 'Leeds Clearing House' online. The application process happens each year with the online system opening for the following year's applications in September and closing in early December. This may vary so please check on the clearing house website for up to date information (www.leeds.ac.uk/chpccp/dates.html).

The applications will be sent to the relevant courses who will then invite applicants to an assessment or interview depending on their selection criteria. The process of assessments and interviews usually begins in February/March of the entry year. Successful applicants will be offered a place on the course that will start at the beginning of the next academic year. For example:

- September 2018 – Clearing House online applications open.
- November 2018 – Clearing House online applications close.
- February to May 2019 – Assessments and interviews are carried out.
- June 2019 – Successful applicants must inform courses of their intention to begin training.
- September/October 2019 – Successful applicants begin training.

Each year the process repeats and if unsuccessful there is opportunity to continue to improve on your work and/or research experience. Each training course has different types of trainees on their course, but there are similar desired competencies such as: communication skills, self-awareness, openness to learning, personal maturity, motivation, warmth, empathy, resilience, organisation, initiative. More information about the application and interview processes is presented in Chapter 5, 'How do I prepare for applications and interviews, and take care of myself?'

How competitive is the course?

For entry to the Doctorate in Clinical Psychology in the UK in 2017, 15% of applicants succeeded in gaining a place on NHS training course as there were 3,932 applications for 594 places. There have been a consistently high number of applicants over the past five years (see Figure 1.1). There are three main reasons for this: firstly, the course is currently funded and UK trainees are paid a salary at Band 6 of the Agenda for Change pay scale during their three years of training. This is the case for the 2018 entry to training but the future funding status for clinical psychology training courses is uncertain. Secondly, clinical psychology training gives people access to a range of different roles that they can undertake which is appealing to many people. Finally, clinical psychology training has high completion rates and there are excellent chances of employment following training. For example, over the past five years between 99 and 99.5% of trainee clinical psychologist pass and complete training. Of the people finishing courses in 2016, 95% took up employment as a clinical psychologist within 12 months of graduating, with 96% of these people working in the NHS or another public sector funded post (Clearing House, 2017).

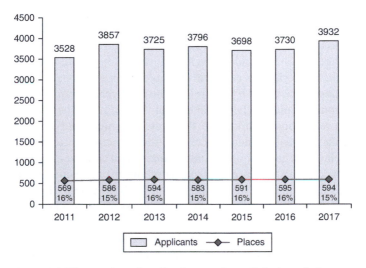

Figure 1.1 The number of applications made to clinical psychology training courses and the number of applicants accepted onto training from 2011 to 2017 (Clearing House, 2017).

Because of the high numbers of applicants, it is common to make multiple application attempts to gain a place on clinical psychology training. Most people who apply to training make two to three applications and the average age to gain a place is 27 years old. The good news is that, as a profession, clinical psychology values people from minority backgrounds and those with varied routes into training. You may have worked in another type of job or been travelling and these experiences could form part of your journey into clinical psychology training. The crucial thing in making the most of these experiences is reflection. You will need to demonstrate the ability to look back on what you have done and think about what you have learnt from these experiences. We will discuss this in much more detail in Chapter 4, 'How can I make the most of my psychology degree and work experience?' and Chapter 5, 'How do I prepare for applications and interviews, and take care of myself?'

WHY PEOPLE CHOOSE NOT TO PURSUE A CAREER IN CLINICAL PSYCHOLOGY

So far, the emphasis has been largely on the positives of working as a clinical psychologist. However, there are several reasons why people may decide that clinical psychology training is not for them. Working as a clinical psychologist is emotionally challenging, particularly if your role involves psychotherapy. There is support in place to help with this but 'burn-out' can be an issue for professionals working in this way (Hannigan, Edwards & Burnard, 2004). In addition to this, the demands on a clinical psychologist in relation to time management and waiting lists can add to this pressure. The impact of austerity and cuts to services means that these demands are unlikely to ease in the near future. For some people, the competitiveness of clinical psychology is off-putting, with 15% of applicants gaining a place each year. The training process is also lengthy compared to other professions; at least six years of study and a minimum of one to two years of work experience, in most cases. For some people, the pay of a clinical psychologist is not enough given the length of time to train and demands of the job. Often people must take on temporary contracts before training because permanent roles are not available, making it difficult for people to feel settled in their personal lives. We consider these challenges and potential alternative careers in Chapter 6, 'How do I know if clinical psychology is for me?'

SUMMARY

You should now have an understanding of what a clinical psychologist is, how they work, why they choose the profession and the route to becoming a clinical psychologist in the UK. Clinical psychologists work in a variety of ways with different people in a range of services and they have varied training helping them to develop their abilities as clinicians, supervisors, consultants, leaders, trainers and researchers. It also means that they're good at forming relationships so are ideal candidates for management and leadership positions within teams. Some of the common myths are that clinical psychologists are the same as psychiatrists, they will try to read your mind or analyse you and that the profession is mumbo-jumbo. We've considered how and why these are myths. The reasons for training as a clinical psychologist are varied and include being interested in the human experience, wanting to understand personal challenges, to pursue a rewarding career, work in varied ways and help people who are distressed.

To train as a clinical psychologist you need to have achieved at least a 2:1 in your undergraduate psychology degree or an equivalent qualification. You also need to have some work experience in a clinical and/or research setting. To obtain a place on a course is competitive and most applicants apply more than once. However, once you do gain a place on training, your chances of gaining a job afterwards are very high. It is important to continue to reflect on and learn from your experiences on your road to training as a clinical psychologist. To help you understand the profession more, we have asked six trainee clinical psychologists and six qualified clinical psychologists to answer some detailed questions which we have presented as 12 profiles.

2

WHAT IS IT LIKE TO TRAIN AS A CLINICAL PSYCHOLOGIST?

In this section, a selection of six trainee profiles are presented, which will give you a detailed insight into the diverse range of experiences of people who are training as a clinical psychologist. Through conversations with people interested in the career, we devised some key questions that we sent to current trainee clinical psychologists. These questions related to their experiences of training, the profession, reasons for training and advice for people considering clinical psychology, amongst other things. This section will provide a summary of their responses which will give you an insight into what it is like to train as a clinical psychologist in the UK.

The trainee psychologists were selected to represent people in different years of training. The information provided here is related to their personal experiences and is not necessarily representative of the experience of other trainee clinical psychologists.

AYESHA'S STORY

Completed by an Asian (Pakistani) female aged 34, who identifies as a Muslim.

What is your current year of training?

Third year trainee clinical psychologist.

Describe the training placements you have worked in.

My first-year placement was in Health Psychology with adults and in a Child and Adolescent Mental Health Service (CAMHS).

My second-year placement was in a Rehabilitation and Recovery (Psychosis) Service and working with older adults. My third-year specialist placement is also in a Child and Adolescent Mental Health Service. The best aspects of the work have included learning about and developing in a variety of areas, such as creative adaptations for therapeutic work with different populations. In addition, working in settings I have not had experience of before with different teams has been eye-opening and challenging in a very positive way. The most challenging aspect for me personally has been the cycle of placements. With the cycle of short placements in the first two years, it felt like you only just got settled in and hit your stride before it was time to start winding down again. The start of placements was most difficult as they were all in new areas and I sometimes felt de-skilled. Reminding myself of the transferable skills I had developed and was continuing to build upon helped with this.

How have you found being on the training course so far?

The interview for the course I am on was quite reflective and not too taxing compared to what some other courses make you do! The worst part was the waiting I think, from application to hearing about interviews, and then to hear of the outcome of interviews. The transition from my previous role to training was a bit difficult. I went from being a fairly autonomous practitioner to a trainee who was going to be constantly evaluated in several ways for three years. I chose this, but don't think I fully appreciated how different it would be until I was a couple of months in. At this point in final year, I believe I have gained a breadth of different skills and experiences which would enable me to work in a variety of settings, both related to clinical psychology and also unrelated. Final year is allowing for more longer-term, in-depth work with clients and also more opportunity to become embedded and work with teams.

Why did you decide to train as a clinical psychologist?

I've always been interested in how people make sense of mental health difficulties. I come from a religious and spiritual background and this plays a large part in how people I know understand distress, which doesn't necessarily always 'fit' with traditional Western understanding. I used to be a CBT therapist and made a career change to pursue clinical psychology. This largely came from wanting to develop in a wider variety of ways than only therapeutically, such as in working with different populations, consultation, supervision, etc. and was also influenced by my work alongside clinical psychologists at the time.

What are your experiences of diversity in the profession?

The stereotype of psychology as white, middle-class and female is still true to a large extent. There is some diversity in terms of age, ethnicity, sexual orientation, socioeconomic status etc. but still noticeably limited, at least on the course I am on. Psychologists are not exempt from the same prejudices, whether conscious or subconscious, than anyone else. Disappointingly, in my experience, bringing awareness to these issues does not mean people are accepting of or willing to consider them as having an impact. However, in my own cohort I have also had positive experiences of my peers being willing to listen and try to understand different viewpoints. I feel a responsibility to speak out about issues that disproportionately impact on some members of society more than others.

If you could give one piece of advice to someone about to pursue a career in clinical psychology, what would it be?

The course isn't the be all and end all. It is training for a job and should be treated as such. There will be plenty of ups and downs like you would expect in any job; don't let the pursuit of getting on the course or, once you are on, the doctorate take over.

What are your interests outside clinical psychology?

I am a bit of an expert in not doing very much in my spare time! Relaxing, reading, going out and holidays all help maintaining a life outside the course.

If you weren't working as a clinical psychologist what would you be doing?

If I wasn't working as a clinical psychologist, I can still see myself working in Mental Health. I would probably still be working therapeutically although more integratively. Either that or I would have pursued a career as a camerawoman for David Attenborough!

MELANIE'S STORY

Completed by a White British female aged 26, who identifies as having no religion.

What is your current year of training?

Second year trainee clinical psychologist.

Describe the training placements you have worked in.

I am currently on placement in an adult Clinical Health Psychology Department. The team is made up of many clinical psychologists, health psychologists, and counsellors working across a range of specialities. The specialities that I am working in are Oncology and Palliative Care. Working with clients who have faced life threatening illnesses and/or are at the end of their lives has provided both challenging and rewarding experiences. The obvious challenge is managing the emotional content of the work, especially if a client passes away. However, I have found myself within a supportive Multi-Disciplinary Team [the different types of professionals that work within a service] and I have really enjoyed working within a team of varying professions. It has been great to gain insight into the different ways in which different professionals support somebody at their end of life. I have also enjoyed exploring, with a client, how they feel their identity has changed after experiencing a life-threatening illness that may also have left them with a long-term disability.

How have you found being on the training course so far?

I was quite lucky in that, at the time of applying for the course, I was working in a department of many clinical psychologists, assistant psychologists and trainee clinical psychologists who were all willing to support me through the application and interview process. It was really helpful to have others look over my application and to discuss potential interview topics with. Coming from a busy assistant psychologist post and from working on psychiatric wards as a support worker, it has been nice to have more 'thinking time' on my placements. I have learnt the importance of taking the time to reflect on the therapeutic process with a client; what is happening in the room and how it is impacting on me personally. Having the space to think about this has helped with my personal and professional development and shape the interventions that I am using.

Why did you decide to train as a clinical psychologist?

As is the same for many people, I have had family members and friends who have experienced difficulties with their mental health at different points in my life. This gave me some insight into the various ways in which people respond to their own mental health, the mental health of others, and the impact it can have on family functioning. I wanted to understand and be a part of the services that are provided to support individuals and their families, and I have always been curious about the psychological theories behind the interventions.

What are your experiences of diversity in the profession?

Working on placements with clients of different culture and faith, I have noticed the importance of having diversity within the work place. I have tried not to feel disadvantaged if I had minimal knowledge of a client's culture and instead ask for information from them or other professionals, e.g. of the same religion or cultural background. This has opened up some really interesting conversations and I have learnt that it is best not to shy away from diversity and the things that make us different. It can be really helpful to acknowledge that we may have little to no knowledge of a client's culture, for example, and ask for more information.

If you could give one piece of advice to someone about to pursue a career in clinical psychology, what would it be?

I'd advise them not to worry about rushing into training. I've really valued all the experiences that I gathered in the time between graduating from my undergraduate degree up until beginning on the course. It provided me with some basic knowledge about service structures within the NHS, how to apply psychological theory in practice and the confidence to interact with teams and with people in distress. On top of this, I found working on wards and with other assistant psychologists really enjoyable!

What are your interests outside clinical psychology?

I really enjoy being creative.

If you weren't working as a clinical psychologist what would you be doing?

Before I went down the route of psychology, I had always deliberated a career in the arts. I've really valued making time to do something creative, e.g. make or paint something, as it helps me to chill out when I'm feeling stressed. I also do yoga and aerial hoop classes which are a really fun way of keeping fit.

PATRICIA'S STORY

Completed by a Black African, female aged 29, who identifies as a Christian

What is your current year of training?

First year trainee clinical psychologist.

Describe the training placements you have worked in.

I am currently on placement at an older adult Inpatient Unit. I have worked with older adults previously but in a research context and with healthy volunteers. I found the transition from working with healthy older adults to working with older adults experiencing acute memory loss very different. It was an eye-opening experience from a personal and clinical perspective. I have enjoyed learning how to communicate and work therapeutically with this client group and their families.

How have you found being on the training course so far?

For me, I feel it has been a long and sometimes hard journey. I loved the clinical experiences I gained but I struggled with the DClinPsy application process. I love my course, it was the only course I wanted. I feel the course fits in with me and my own morals and values. Training has been difficult and at times I feel 'I don't know anything'. I constantly feel like 'I am consciously incompetent'. Nevertheless, training has taught me about myself and reminded me that I am here to learn and it's ok to feel this way!

Why did you decide to train as a clinical psychologist?

From a very young age I'd always felt different that people didn't quite understand me, or I didn't fit in. It was through my personal experiences and my own interest in learning about different contexts that sparked my passion and enthusiasm. I did Sociology as an A-level but was persuaded by my parents to do a joint honours degree; that's when I first found psychology! Since then, I felt 'housed', i.e. I was learning about myself and other people in a very different way. I then continued to look for opportunities, which was the most difficult part of my journey, to develop and guide my career options.

What are your experiences of diversity in the profession?

I personally find this a difficult question to answer. On the one hand my experiences of diversity from an ethnicity point of view has been limited. I have often been the only if not one of a very small group of people from the same ethnic group in my working environment. I found this experience difficult sometimes. Perhaps this was a new environment and I felt alone. In hindsight, this has been a big learning experience to understand myself and my strengths. It has also enabled curiosity to understand the reasons behind this and what I could do to help. Equally, learning that we work with diversity every day and between us all share differences and similarities and it is this that empowers growth and lived experiences. It has not been an easy journey, but I'd say use every experience as a learning curve to foster and shape your own identity.

If you could give one piece of advice to someone about to pursue a career in clinical psychology, what would it be?

I would describe a career in clinical psychology as a boxing ring; you may get knocked down along the way, and it may hurt and be a painful experience, but courage is getting back up and learning from the experience. Passion, perseverance and commitment will be your strength.

MICHAEL'S STORY

Completed by a White British male aged 27, who identifies as having no religion.

What is your current year of training?

Third year trainee clinical psychologist.

Describe the training placements you have worked in.

I am currently based in a Recovery Team. Other placements have included an Assessment and Brief Treatment Team, Child and Adolescent Mental Health Services and Health Psychology. my next placement will be with in a Forced Migration Trauma Service. The most challenging aspects of the work I have found is the responsibility that comes with it. I often believe that I can help everyone, at least somehow, that comes into my therapy room. It's a hopeful position I take with everyone, but with 'unsuccessful' cases I can't help but feel is down to personal failings, e.g. not knowing enough, not running sessions well enough, failing to engage people etc. At many points, I have found myself sitting there having no idea what I meant to be doing and wondering how I have made it so far without anyone realising. On the flip side of this, when the work goes well, or you have connected well with someone, it feels very rewarding. I share in the success, I guess. Imagery work, particularly with trauma, has stuck with the most. Which again, can be a double-edged sword. For one, it is often successful and you can see great results, e.g. the nightmares have gone. But on the other side, I now have those memories too and they can pop up in my mind at unexpected times.

How have you found being on the training course so far?

The application process was very stressful. I was fortunate enough to get on the first time I applied, and was really only doing a 'practice year', a common thing we tell ourselves the first time to take the blow out of being unsuccessful, I think. However, afterwards I appreciated that it would be a very aversive experience to repeat again. The waiting for news at each stage was probably the worst part, as it generally takes place over several months, it is hard to plan life. Especially knowing that if you are not successful, you need a plan for a year just to go through that waiting process again. I got only one interview. Preparing for it was difficult, partially because the course interview is deliberately set-up to examine how you think and respond. I ended up reading a lot of books and articles, of which absolutely none I used in the interview. The best advice I got at the time was to be friendly, take time to think, and plan how to respond to questions, rather than focus on content. The transition was fine, I thought it was a good balance of working and studying which I initially enjoyed. By now, in third year, I have had enough with studying and would like to get back into working full-time. I have spoken to people trying to get on the course and doing applications, and they have asked me about the 'What would you like to get out of training' section. On reflection, I have not gained anything new and discrete, but more of a continuation of a process that started when I was assistant, that is, reflexive thinking, interpersonal skills, psychological theory and its application. Training has been a very positive experience but there has not been anything unexpected in it. These are all processes that should begin before applying.

Why did you decide to train as a clinical psychologist?

I decided I wanted to be a psychologist at a young age, in secondary school. I can't recall the exact reason and, if I am being completely honest, I chose it long before I even knew what it was or whether I would be any good at it. Probably because it sounded prestigious and my friends seemed to know exactly what they wanted to do, so I should pick something as well (as an aside, none of my friends ended up in the careers they picked). It wasn't until I did a placement year as part of my undergraduate degree where I worked as an honorary assistant psychologist did I get any inkling of what it was. I suppose I got lucky in this regard, that I picked something that I would be passionate about and actually be okay at.

My honorary assistant post was brilliant at learning the basics and meeting people. It was the start of developing a therapy 'style' and I recommend anyone doing a degree to do a placement year, not in the least because you probably won't be able to afford it after university (I certainly could not). Otherwise just general life experiences have generally prepared me. I was one of the unfortunate few who was forced to grow up relatively young as I had a period of homelessness and sofa surfing when I was 16/17, which ended when I went to go do my degree. This certainly helped me to mature and gave me an empathetic understanding of people I would meet who were also going through difficult times. Although it is worth adding that it also gave me some biases that I have been careful to be reflective about in my work. Self-awareness is key to working well with people accessing services.

What are your experiences of diversity in the profession?

I have had held two pre-training roles; one honorary assistant psychologist position and one assistant psychologist position. The first was a very white population all round, I can't recall any diversity in terms of ethnicity in either the staff or service users, although there was the usual divide often found in mental health in terms of class. The second was the opposite, being in a very diverse area, the majority were not White British, and the majority had experienced poverty. There was also larger diversity with religion, sexuality and culture and I learnt a lot while being there. The psychologists I worked with were diverse in themselves, all different ethnically, positions on sexuality, professional background. Saying that, I am still yet to meet a black male clinical psychologist. I have also been involved in the widening access scheme to mentor those from Black Minority Ethnic (BME) backgrounds into clinical psychology, hopefully I will continue this.

If you could give one piece of advice to someone about to pursue a career in clinical psychology, what would it be?

While it is good to be looking forward towards the Doctorate in Clinical Psychology, it should not be at the expense of whatever position you are in. Like I mentioned earlier the process of becoming a good psychologist begins long before the course, so it is important that you make the most of where you are now. Take on as much experience as you can, try to integrate psychological ways of thinking and working into whatever you are doing, and be reflective. The course is only a course at the end of the day, when you join it should be nothing 'new', but a continuation. From an anecdotal perspective, I have found those who direct all their energy in getting on the course often put it on a pedestal and often aren't successful. Those who have a realistic perspective on the course are often more successful.

What are your interests outside clinical psychology?

A mixture of things. I enjoy programming as a hobby, and am involved in a few slightly geeky things, e.g. moderating forums, making game mods, running stalls at convention shows. Of course, reading, socialising, drinking too much, eating too much, are enough said.

If you weren't working as a clinical psychologist what would you be doing?

If I didn't do this I would have likely pursed something in programming. I am glad I didn't, I should add, as I think the other advantage of clinical psychology is that really expands and improves you as a person. It makes you think about the kind of person you want to be and the kind of life you want to live.

ELODIE'S STORY

Completed by a White British female aged 32, who identifies as having no religion.

What is your current year of training?

Second year trainee clinical psychologist.

Describe the training placements you have worked in.

In my first year of training I was based in a Secondary Care Adult Mental Health Service for people who have been given a diagnosis of personality disorder. The challenges of working in this area were trying to engage with this client group; the service experiences a high number of people who do not attend and drop outs, which as a trainee can be frustrating and knock your confidence. Also, the clients often presented with high levels of risk, which needed to be managed. However, the work was very rewarding and when clients did engage with the service it was amazing to see the changes they could make to their lives. I also found that in working in this area I developed a greater understanding and empathy for the client group.

How have you found being on the training course so far?

I found the application form really challenging to complete. The limited character count and being unsure of what courses would be looking for in an application made it feel very much like I was guessing what might make a good application form. Having the chance to read previous application forms was really helpful and getting advice from my service lead, who was a clinical psychologist, helped. The process of preparing for the interviews was stressful and I was lucky to know someone on the courses at one of the institutions I interviewed at, so I was able to find out a bit more about what to expect on the day. Going over previous year's interview questions was useful as was speaking to people who had had interviews previously, whether successful or not. The interviews on the day, although anxiety provoking, were generally positive experiences. I found staff and students I met supportive, interested and compassionate. Transitioning onto clinical training was emotionally challenging in a way I had not expected. I had thought I would find the academic side, returning to a whole day of lectures, the most challenging aspect. However, the course I am on managed this very well and doesn't require trainees to submit any work until after Christmas of the first year. Instead, I found the main challenge was meeting so many new people. Spending all day with a large number of other people who don't know each other and making friends felt reminiscent of starting undergraduate study again! I found it quite overwhelming at times and I felt exhausted but thought that I needed to present a smiley, friendly face. However, after a few weeks I started to feel more settled.

Why did you decide to train as a clinical psychologist?

At university, I had been mainly interested in developmental psychology and so decided to go into teaching. I worked as a teaching assistant in a primary school for a year but realised that I missed using my psychological knowledge more explicitly. I decided then to apply for a Postgraduate Certificate in Education, specialising in social science teaching. After being accepted onto this course and completing my training, I spent four years working in a secondary school in London, teaching psychology. Over this time, I learnt a lot of skills that I think helped me prepare for work as a clinical psychologist; in particular, I gained management experience and team working skills. I learnt to think about more than just the individual student in terms of factors that might be affecting someone's school attendance and performance. I learnt how to sit in a room with a raging teenager and be okay with that! It was seeing young people I taught struggle with their own mental health issues that made me want to change career and try to get onto the Doctorate in Clinical Psychology. I thought, naively, that I could do more to effect change as a psychologist for young people, than I could as a teacher. So, I applied for the Psychological Wellbeing Practitioner Training and then worked in Improving Access to Psychological Therapies for three years. This gave me a real insight into the pressures the NHS is under and I developed my clinical skills in this role. Furthermore, I learnt to manage with a high caseload and organise my time and different responsibilities within this role effectively. This is something I have definitely needed as a trainee clinical psychologist. Also, learning the art of leaving work at work and ensuring time to look after myself!

What are your experiences of diversity in the profession?

I feel that within teaching there was more diversity, but even so still predominantly White British and mainly female. The further along my career in clinical psychology that I have got the less diverse my experiences have been. Now working within a Multi-Disciplinary Team, I feel there is more diversity across the different professions, but my experience of clinical psychology so far has been that it is not very diverse.

If you could give one piece of advice to someone about to pursue a career in clinical psychology, what would it be?

Choose experiences that you think you will enjoy and that will interest you, not just things that you think will look good on an application.

What are your interests outside clinical psychology?

Playing football, doing yoga, going to the theatre, going to comedy gigs, reading and other things not related to psychology such as spending time with friends. Nothing that out of the ordinary!

If you weren't working as a clinical psychologist what would you be doing?

If I wasn't a clinical psychologist, I would probably still be in teaching, working as a head of year (I would hope) or maybe I would have eventually gone into educational psychology.

SHEENA'S STORY

Completed by an Arab female aged 26, who identifies as a Muslim.

What is your current year of training?

Second year trainee clinical psychologist.

Describe the training placements you have worked in.

I worked in a private hospital for my first year of training. This work was very varied. I mainly did CBT while drawing on other modalities (Dialectical Behaviour Therapy, Schema Therapy and Mindfulness) while working with a range of presentations. It was interesting to work in a private setting, as it often highlighted issues of power and privilege, particularly in relation to class. At the time of writing this, I am in a six-month placement at a Child and Adolescent Mental Health Service. This work is integrative as it draws on CBT as well as systemic theory and application, and I learned to also formulate from a psychodynamic perspective. The best aspects are of course seeing clients get better, the variety and I very much enjoy learning about different theories in lectures and then going on to apply them in the therapy room. The most challenging aspect, especially initially, was the emotional toll it took on me to hear people's stories. However, with supervision and reflection this was turned into something to be used positively, for both clients and myself as one continues with their personal and professional development. Another challenging aspect is perhaps holding in mind different models and knowing when to draw on which. This is a skill that I have heard comes with time!

How have you found being on the training course so far?

Applications and interviews were of course a nerve-wracking time. I got on second time around and while the initial 'rejection' was a blow, it definitely contributed to my growth and development, and allowed me to know what to expect second time. I found that when I learned to accept that all those pre-training jobs and experience were all just part of the journey, and to slow down and not rush into getting on (easier said than done, I know) then everything just became much easier.

Initially, it was overwhelming, lots of new faces, information, deadlines and placements but it was very much supported by the fact that everyone else is in the same boat and the training course was very supportive at the outset. It has been just over a year on since I started, and I feel that I am a very different person already, and I know many others on the course share this sentiment. It is a steep transition, and certainly throws you in at the deep end but you do learn to float!

I have gained a lot from training so far. Academically, I feel so much more knowledgeable about different theories and approaches. Clinically, I am more confident, and I am understanding myself and other people better. I feel I am now better equipped to navigate professional relationships and understand systems that impact on people's wellbeing. I have enjoyed meeting so many amazing, like-minded people with a diverse range of skills and experiences.

Why did you decide to train as a clinical psychologist?

I was always fascinated in how people think and why, from a young age. I was a very inquisitive young girl, going around asking everyone what they were thinking whenever they got into a daydream! Witnessing mental health difficulties and disabilities within my family and community, in the context of a culture where speaking about such things is taboo and stigmatised made me want to change that. I have a strong interest in stigma in relation to mental health and learning disabilities, as well as the construction of both in different cultures and religions. I did research in these areas before training and I loved it. Also, my first clinical experience was at a service for refugees who had experienced trauma. It was very difficult as a first clinical experience, but equally rewarding and it further sparked my commitment to work towards a career in clinical psychology. I think seeing how varied the work can be, with clinical, research and academic components, really helped me to make my decision as I get bored very quickly.

What are your experiences of diversity in the profession?

During my education, I was aware of under-representation in terms of culture and ethnicity. I was very interested in doing my own dissertation as an undergrad in Arab psychology. My supervisor was very open and supportive about this. Pre-training I started gaining research experience in an academic setting where there was a lot of under-representation in terms of fellow staff members and I was very conscious of this, particularly in relation to ethnicity, culture and religion. I think the main way I felt the under-representation impacted me pre-training was not having as much access to friends or family members who actually knew what clinical psychology was, which initially felt rather isolating and added another layer of difficulty to getting on training. However, I can say that I was very fortunate in that I had fantastic mentors and supervisors who were very aware and critical of this under-representation and were also devoted to change that.

Pre-training, I worked on the Widening Access to Clinical Psychology Scheme as an assistant psychologist. In researching diversity in the profession as part of my role, I did come across some shocking figures in terms of under-representation across the country. Having said that, I also got to evaluate and be part of some wonderful initiatives to increase diversity such as the mentoring scheme and workshops. During training, I'm one of the champions of the widening access scheme as I really experienced its benefits, both personally and professionally.

I would say the main challenge I've had in relation to diversity during training is in terms of religion. I think there seems to be huge under-representation in relation to religion. This has been highlighted to me in the way I have sometimes heard clinicians talk about spiritual or religious clients. I feel that it is often misunderstood and spun in a negative light. I've heard clinicians talk about clients' religious or spiritual beliefs as 'barriers' to therapy, rather than core values informed by the clients' world view to be curious about, respected and worked with.

If you could give one piece of advice to someone about to pursue a career in clinical psychology, what would it be?

Do not give up! Don't listen to all the horror stories about the difficulties of getting on, sadly they always overpower the success stories. See all the experiences you're gaining as part of the journey. Get on the widening access scheme. Be yourself and embrace your own diversity, as we all have diversity and we all represent something in some way, that way you're being authentic, and you will stand out.

What are your interests outside clinical psychology?

I love to do Arabic calligraphy, read and travel with friends.

If you weren't working as a clinical psychologist what would you be doing?

My ideal vision right now of what I would be doing if the doctorate became a figment of my imagination would be to spend time travelling in between South America, where I would become fluent in Spanish while teaching English to disadvantaged groups and beach hopping, and Istanbul, where I would become a pro at Arabic calligraphy and drink Turkish coffee all day. A more realistic alternative would probably be doing research in global mental health to raise awareness and challenge stigma of mental health and learning disabilities in low- and middle-income countries.

SUMMARY

The trainee clinical psychologists had a range of experiences on their placements so far. They had chosen a variety of reasons for becoming a clinical psychologist and their experiences had varied greatly. Their experiences of diversity in the profession were mixed but there was a sense that clinical psychology training could be more diverse. Their advice for aspiring clinical psychologists was about making the most of your experience and persisting even though the process can be very challenging. The trainee clinical psychologists had a wide range of interests outside of clinical psychology and a number of them have some creative talent. The trainee clinical psychologists provided a lot of information about their own personal journeys into the career. Remember the following advice for inspiration and encouragement along your own journey:

- *There will be many of highlights and challenges like you would expect in any career journey. Try not to allow the pursuit of obtaining a place on the course take over your life.*
- *The process of getting onto the training course does not need to be rushed. It is worth making the most of all the experiences that you gather in the time between graduating from your undergraduate degree up until beginning on the course and beyond that* (we'll consider this more in Chapter 4, 'How can I make the most of my psychology degree and work experience?').
- *Becoming a 'good' psychologist is a process that starts even before the course begins. Try to make use of psychological ways of understanding issues into the variety of things you are doing. Also remember to reflect on your work and the way you interact with it, to continue to develop as a psychologist.*
- *Use all of the experiences of adversity and challenges along the way to foster and shape your own unique identity as a psychologist. Maintaining passion, perseverance and commitment to the work will be help you develop resilience.*
- *Choose job roles and work experiences that interest you and have the potential to add to your knowledge and skill set, rather than things that you think will appear more 'favourable' on an application.*

NOTE

Clinical psychology courses continue to develop ways of improving diversity in the clinical psychologists that they train. The above trainee clinical psychologists were selected because they provide a diverse representation in relation to gender and ethnicity/cultural background.

3

WHAT IS IT LIKE TO WORK AS A CLINICAL PSYCHOLOGIST?

This selection of six profiles will give you an insight in to the diverse range of experiences of people who are working as clinical psychologists in a range of services in the UK. These questions were related to their experiences of qualified life, the profession, reasons for training and advice for people considering clinical psychology, amongst other things. This section will provide a useful insight into what it is like to work as a clinical psychologist.

The clinical psychologists were selected based on their area of speciality, as the role of a clinical psychologist can vary greatly between services. The clinical psychologists were working in Forensic Psychology Services, Paediatric Health Psychology, Adult Mental Health, Neuropsychology and Learning Disability Services. As with the trainee profiles, the information provided here is related to their personal experiences and is not necessarily representative of the experience of other clinical psychologists.

PETER'S STORY

Completed by a White British male aged 28, who identifies as an atheist.

How long have you been qualified?

Three years.

What is your area of speciality?

Forensic (Criminal Justice) Services.

Describe the current post you are working in.

I currently work in a Forensic Service, primarily as a Multi-Disciplinary Team (MDT) member on a low secure assessment and treatment ward and as an MDT member in a Forensic Outreach Team. The aspect of the work that I value the most is trying to make sense of difficult to understand experiences and actions, through conversations with service users and with staff. The aspect of the work that I find most challenging is managing the personal and systemic anxieties associated with working in forensics [these are the worries that people within the organisation or team have which results from several complex factors].

How have you found being qualified so far?

I initially applied for qualified posts in Adult Psychological Therapies Services and found the process difficult, as I was often told, during interview feedback, that I was competing against Band 7s [a pay grade for clinical psychologists, which is part of the Agenda for Change pay scale] taking sideways steps. I don't think that my experiences during training or my preferred approach at the time helped in getting that type of post either, so I decided to apply for a job more in line with my experiences during training. I found the first 18 months in qualified work difficult, as I experienced the responsibility of being involved in decisions about risk management very anxiety-provoking. However, over time, I think that I have become more pragmatic [practical] and less idealistic in my thinking, perhaps also learning to more appropriately manage my expectations about the limits of my influence.

Why did you decide to train as a clinical psychologist?

Experiences of personal and family mental health problems certainly influenced my decision to train as a clinical psychologist. Before training, I think that I emphasised the latter and an associated wish to help others. However, over time, I have come to think that my decision to train was more influenced by questions about my own mental health. I think that, generally, I always tending to be curious about others' experiences and tending to put myself in positions to listen to others' experiences has been the best preparation for work as a qualified clinical psychologist. I still consider curious listening to be the key skill required.

What are your experiences of diversity in the profession?

The main reflection on my own experiences, in relation to diversity, is that I attended an all-boys school from the ages of 7 until 18 and, subsequently, have trained and worked in majority-female Psychology Departments, since beginning my undergraduate degree. I have become more aware over time of the biases in my thinking, in relation to gender, and have been grateful to have had open conversations with colleagues about gendered assumptions in the workplace. I have become gradually more preoccupied with the relative lack of ethnic and socio-economic diversity in the profession, since qualifying. I have been considering this more problematic, since I have been thinking more about the dynamics of power in Forensic Services and in Mental Health Services in general.

If you could give one piece of advice to someone about to pursue a career in clinical psychology, what would it be?

Despite the pressure to demonstrate that you are capable and competent before, during and after training, do whatever you can to hold onto enough uncertainty and doubt to be able to genuinely learn from service users and from colleagues.

What are your interests outside clinical psychology?

Outside of work, I love spending time with my partner, my friends and my family. I also love reading non-fiction and am currently trying to get to grips with pragmatic philosophy. I also enjoy film, so I try to get to the cinema when possible, and music, particularly classical. Hearing live classical music is one of my favourite things to do.

If you weren't working as a clinical psychologist what would you be doing?

If I wasn't a clinical psychologist, I would like to either practice law or to go back into academia.

ALICE'S STORY

Completed by a White British female aged 32, who identifies as an atheist.

How long have you been qualified?

Three years.

What is your area of speciality?

Paediatric Health Psychology.

Describe the current post you are working in.

I work in a children's hospital in the Endocrine Team. I meet with young people and their families at different stages of their illness and time in hospital. We meet to talk about a young person's diagnosis, what it means for their life, and how they might cope with the challenges that that illness might present. I also work a lot with parents and teams to think about how illness affects everyone in a young person's system and how we all have different ways of responding to that. It is a real privilege to work with young people and their families, and see the many ways that people cope with challenges and difficulties. At the hospital every day is different, and you get to work with families as inpatients, outpatients and a lot of support over the phone, due to the distance they live from the hospital. My preferred way of working is systemic, and the hospital naturally lends itself to this way of working. I work a lot with staff teams to formulate patients and their family's strengths and difficulties. One of the challenging aspects of the role is that it can be very busy! Due to the nature of seeing inpatients, outpatients and teams, diaries change so much day to day depending on the patient's condition and need. As with many psychology roles, working in a hospital with illness can be distressing and whilst it is a privilege to be with families at that time, it can take an emotional toll. Having supportive colleagues and supervisors is really important to support you with that.

How have you found being qualified so far?

I found the process of getting assistant jobs very tough, but have found it a fairer and, dare I say, an easier process to get qualified roles. The application process draws on skills that you are using in your current post and as your experience starts to build it is clearer what posts are desirable to you and what experience you need to get them. I loved being a trainee psychologist and the diverse placements you have is so interesting and you are constantly learning. I found it difficult to always be the 'new trainee' in the team, and feeling that just as you got settled into a team you were moving onto a new placement. I had a 12-month placement at my current place of work for my final placement and then took a post here as my first qualified job. It helped taking a post where I already felt familiar with the work and the team. The team were also great at seeing me as a qualified psychologist once I took the post; I think that could be difficult in other roles where you may still be seen as a trainee. For me the biggest change from trainee to qualified psychologist was the increase in workload and not having the protection of the university monitoring how busy you are. I feel I have gained so much practicing as a qualified clinical psychologist, both personally and professionally. Professionally, I have always been interested in systemic ways of working, but over the years I have realised that without thinking about people's lives in context and within the systems that they live, then our ability to help or change anything is very limited. Personally, I have learned a lot about myself and my identity and why some cases seem to affect me more than others, and my own needs.

Why did you decide to train as a clinical psychologist?

From when I was very young I wanted to be in some kind of 'helping' profession, whether that be a teacher or a doctor or a nurse. I really enjoyed psychology for A-level but hadn't really thought about pursuing anything in the field. I took a gap year between college and university as I was really stuck with what I wanted to study and why, and during this time I worked as a phlebotomist in a hospital. I loved meeting so many different people, of different ages and backgrounds each day. I also loved working in the hospital but felt that many of the jobs within a hospital require a focus on one particular aspect of a person; so often the dominant medical condition. I enjoyed getting to know what people liked, their hobbies, who and what was important to them, their hopes, etc. Researching jobs at this time I thought a psychologist would be a role where I could see someone holistically and work in a field which sounded fascinating. I worked in different caring roles in dementia care homes, and children's respite centres and loved working in these areas.

What are your experiences of diversity in the profession?

I really struggled when I was training that people in my cohort might say that 'we are not a diverse cohort because most us are white and middle-class'. It felt very difficult that diversity seemed to be based on visible differences between people, and silenced those less visible differences. I did not identify with a 'middle-class' background, and found it very difficult to speak about this. I found it difficult to have a voice often in larger group activities and wondered whether this might have come from me having not being used to public speaking based on my education at that point. I found that my voice grew in confidence when I qualified as I became more confident with my abilities and knowledge through working. I also think that not having a privileged upbringing has meant that I am more curious and empathetic with the people I work with around this.

If you could give one piece of advice to someone about to pursue a career in clinical psychology, what would it be?

Keep going! I think it is really tough to keep applying and not know when you might be accepted onto training. I also think it is so important to not put life on hold, all the experiences you have before training will help so much and are never wasted.

If you weren't working as a clinical psychologist what would you be doing?

I love photography and often think if I wasn't a psychologist maybe I would want to pursue this more. I love running, cycling and yoga, keeping fit is really important to me, I also feel very lucky to have an 'able' body that allows me to push it to its limits.

LINA'S STORY

Completed by an Asian female aged 47, who identifies as having no religion, but has a Hindu background.

How long have you been qualified?

18 years.

What is your area of speciality?

Adult Mental Health.

Describe the current post you are working in.

I currently work in Adult Mental Health in Rehabilitation Services and Acute Inpatient Services. I enjoy my clinical contact with service users, though this is not as frequent as it once was, listening to their stories, understanding what has led to them being involved with Mental Health Services and finding a way of being an ally with them. I enjoy the clinical leadership aspect of my job; supporting and driving clinical innovation that will contribute to a service user's and family's recovery, whatever their end goal might be. Finally, I also enjoy the strategic elements of my post; being in a position to influence services or an organisation to think and be more psychological in its approach. The most challenging aspect of my job is working in a cultural, political and financial climate and context that isn't always compassionate. I find it difficult that often decisions are made about efficiency and effectiveness (rightly so) without any consideration of the personal or human cost involved. As the rhetoric is about business I find that this becomes translated into some Health Services as not needing to be thoughtful or reflective about the implications of decisions.

How have you found being qualified so far?

I can't imagine doing anything else but being a clinical psychologist so despite the challenges I wouldn't swap my job or profession. There have been opportunities to move ahead in my career to take on a more corporate role, but I have resisted. Following clinical training, I hadn't had an interview for three years so the step up to a qualified interview was daunting. However, I qualified at a time when there were many jobs for clinical psychologists available and not much competition, so I found the only interview I had was more of a conversation about my specialist interests and about which service, in the NHS Trust, I wanted to work in, so it was a very pleasant surprise. My first post was a split post in Community Mental Health Team (CMHT) and an Assertive Outreach Service (AO). I was part of a Psychology Team in the CMHT, so the transition was easy as I was given support and continued professional development time every week. The AO Service had never had a clinical psychologist before, so I was given a free hand to develop the role of a psychologist. Though I found this an exciting opportunity, I wasn't surrounded by other psychologists which was challenging at times. There were times when I wasn't sure I knew what I was doing, in the first six months post-qualification, but my supervisor, an eminent psychologist in psychosis, shared with me that it took him five years before he felt that he had established himself as a clinical psychologist and that really helped me turn a corner in my thinking. It allowed me to take the pressure off myself and allow the transition to happen naturally.

As a clinical psychologist, I've gained a better understanding and appreciation of the strength and fragility of the human spirit and the importance of relationships and reputation in non-clinical aspects of my post.

Why did you decide to train as a clinical psychologist?

I made a decision at the age of 15 to pursue a career in clinical psychology. At the time, I'm not sure why except something about the description of the discipline helped to click other experiences in place; somehow it made sense. Looking back, I think being brought up in a coal mining village strongly influenced my identity/identities: the personal experience of prejudice, the impact of the miner's strike of the 1980s on families and the community and the recognition of my privilege, compared to my neighbours, of educational and financial mobility. Injustice and inequality has shaped me, and I think I was looking (unconsciously) for a career that represented my personal and political values. However, it wasn't until I discovered Community Psychology in my clinical training that the final piece of the jigsaw came together.

What are your experiences of diversity in the profession?

I didn't know any clinical psychologists before I decided to pursue this as a career, so I didn't really have a conception of how representative the profession was. I completed work experience at a day centre for people with psychosis in sixth form and all the psychologists attached to the hospital were White British, so I had an indication that the profession might predominantly be also. However, as most of my life I had lived in a social, political and cultural context of White British dominance this did not pose any challenges for me. This was the status quo and I accepted it, as such, at the time.

I trained at a course where there were 25 trainees in each year and most were female and White British. My training year was more diverse in that I was one of three Asian women and there were also three men. Most trainees were of average age for clinical training, with a couple of people with a prior career in nursing. There was also diversity in terms of privilege and social class background in the year. I haven't experienced any challenges in my professional life in terms of diversity, apart from the odd service user not wanting to work with me, and in fact it was a comment by a professor of clinical psychology during my undergraduate degree about how the profession needed more people like me, related to my ethnicity, that spurred me on.

If you could give one piece of advice to someone about to pursue a career in clinical psychology, what would it be?

Think carefully about why you want to enter the field and whether it is clinical psychology that you specifically want to choose, mainly due to the current challenges to the profession and the context of the NHS. Think about what you can bring to the profession that will support its development.

What are your interests outside clinical psychology?

I spend my spare time doing things that help me to switch off from work like being with friends and family, whilst also having some alone time, usually with a book. I like art forms like sculpture, film, theatre and photography and dabble in a bit of photography myself.

If you weren't working as a clinical psychologist what would you be doing?

If I wasn't a clinical psychologist I'm not sure what I would be doing but it would definitely be in the public sector.

JAMES' STORY

Completed by a White British male aged 30, who identifies as a Christian.

How long have you been qualified?

Two years.

What is your area of speciality?

Neuropsychological Rehabilitation.

Describe the current post you are working in.

I currently work in a Rehabilitation Service for people with complex needs following neurological illness, injury and poly-trauma, and work with people both as inpatients and in the community after discharge. The variety of work in the job is a great strength of the post, but this also represents a significant challenge to understand the wide range of presentations we see, particularly when there is a functional overlay to a neurological diagnosis. By virtue of the complex needs of our patients, aspects of the work take place in a hospital-centric environment and this can be a particular challenge due to the medical hierarchy in place, however the MDT generally supports and values the unique contribution of clinical psychology. I generally have a good amount of autonomy within my current role so can contribute to service development and research projects alongside my clinical work without *too* much of an impact on my work life balance. I am also fortunate to work closely with a small team of clinical psychologists so have good local options for peer support.

How have you found being qualified so far?

I managed to secure this post halfway through my final year of training so knowing that I had been offered a permanent contract in an interesting field was a great motivator during those difficult last six months on the course where you are balancing a challenging placement, a thesis and trying to keep on top of real life. I was initially anxious about the prospect of applying for a job after training as I had already begun to have flashbacks to trying to get an assistant psychologist post, however I was pleasantly surprised that I was offered an interview for all of the clinical posts I applied for. I felt well prepared for the interviews through my learning on the course and placements and only had to do some preparation work on policy and governance issues relevant to the specific area. The interviews were objectively challenging, but my subjective experience was that they were fairly relaxed with none of the power dynamics and abject stress of assistant/trainee interviews; much more like a conversation amongst your peers, which was refreshing.

The transition from training to qualification has been a generally positive experience for me. My work-life balance is largely improved, and it has taken some time to remember what normal people do when they come home from work rather than having to plunge all my time into the thesis or exam revision. I found that I have missed the regular contact with my training cohort, but this was largely ameliorated by joining a team of supportive, energised clinical psychologists. It has been an odd experience suddenly having a significant level of clinical responsibility and being unable to rely on the phrase 'I'll check with my supervisor' in times of crisis, however this transition has not been too traumatic within my current post as I have been lucky to have had good support from psychology and other colleagues. I have had a couple of episodes where I have felt slightly out of my depth, however I am mindful that I work in a fairly unconventional setting for clinical psychology and there are many aspects of my work that were not covered by the doctorate programme, which has required some additional supervision and training post-qualification. My main transitional challenge has been to relax and slow down the pace of my work as training instils in you the need to finish all your work within a tidy six-month window.

So far, I have enjoyed being a qualified clinical psychologist and still allow myself brief episodes of smugness when I think back to how all of this seemed unobtainable back when I was desperate to get clinical experience after my undergraduate degree. This smugness is well balanced by the occasional bout of imposter syndrome. I've yet to metamorphosise into this mythical all-knowing, all-confident clinical psychologist but I'm generally content with doing a good enough job of it at the moment.

Why did you decide to train as a clinical psychologist?

A lot of the men in my family have worked in engineering so I was brought up to be curious and to find enjoyment in trying to understand how things fit together. I originally considered going into law or medicine as I enjoyed taking an analytical approach to problem solving. I think I was initially drawn towards studying psychology as a way to understand some of the uncertainty I was experiencing following a series of issues with my own mental health in my teens and early 20s and my mixed experiences of receiving help. I decided that I wanted to work towards clinical training after working as a support worker for a few years in a residential unit for people with brain injuries. I felt really out of my comfort zone when I started this job, but I enjoyed trying to work out how to best support someone with multiple complex needs. It was also just an enormous privilege to be a witness to people trying to rebuild their bodies, minds and lives following a traumatic life changing event. It felt good to be a small part of their story.

What are your experiences of diversity in the profession?

I am a heterosexual white male from a relatively comfortable background and have no misgivings about this providing me with certain opportunities in life that people from other backgrounds have been unable to access. I have tried to use my experiences as a man who has personal experience of mental health difficulties within my own clinical practice to promote engagement and challenge the prevailing discourse that 'men don't want to talk about their problems'. I was very conscious of a lack of visible diversity in my training cohort and have significant concerns about this becoming entrenched further in the context of proposed funding changes to the training programmes. I am relieved, however, that our training provides us with the reflexivity [the ability to think about what is happening and to change your approach] to understand how our sociodemographic characteristics can impact on how our clients perceive us individually and as a helping profession. I was a little concerned about starting my current job as I work in the same city where I grew up and my accent marks me out as coming from a particularly middle-class postcode, but generally this has not been an issue as most of the patients I work with are just relieved to have access to support.

If you could give one piece of advice to someone about to pursue a career in clinical psychology, what would it be?

Relax. I think the idea that you just need to be 'good enough' is the single most liberating thing I have learnt, both about being a clinical psychologist and about being a human being. The sheer level of competitiveness to get an assistant post or to get onto a doctorate programme is, in my opinion, not representative of the attitude required to make the most of a career in clinical psychology. That is not to say that I've mastered this as this point in my career; it's widely accepted that we often don't follow the advice we give to others!

What are your interests outside clinical psychology?

I enjoy hiking, photography and being outside as I find I need to make a conscious effort to shift my thinking away from my day to day routine and remember that there is more to life.

If you weren't working as a clinical psychologist what would you be doing?

If clinical psychology did not exist I would still want to be doing a job where I can help people, something like a science educator post in a museum or national park. Or a travel writer with a massive grant from *The Guardian*.

NADIA'S STORY

Completed by an Asian (Pakistani) female aged 29, who identifies as a Muslim.

How long have you been qualified?

One year.

What is your area of speciality?

Adult Learning Disabilities.

Describe the current post you are working in.

I work in a Community Adult Learning Disability Team. My role is incredibly varied, I see people for assessments, that include cognitive assessments, and use of psychometrics to determine eligibility for the service. I also see people for individual one-to-one therapeutic work, predominantly using a systemic and narrative framework. I am part of the reflecting team in family therapy sessions; I conduct staff consultations and network meetings, alongside running groups, and working with carers. I am also involved in running a research project. The variety is the best aspect of the work, which keeps the role interesting. I am constantly learning and growing as a psychologist, and that is something I value and enjoy.

The most challenging aspect of the work is with working in an MDT. It can be challenging explaining the role of psychology within the team as beyond having 'difficult conversations' with people. I personally find it frustrating needing to explain the benefit of psychological input repeatedly. Whilst this is not a major problem, and on the whole the team understands and respects the role of psychology, there have been a few isolated incidents that create challenges requiring careful thought and consideration in order to manage, while maintaining positive working relationships with the team.

How have you found being qualified so far?

Qualified life has been interesting thus far. The autonomy is liberating whilst also can feel isolating at times. I appreciate the support available to me within my service, including one-to-one supervision, and specific modality-based supervision. However, I am aware that this is substantially less than the support I had as a trainee, where I felt sheltered and protected for most of my placements. Additionally, being a part of a cohort and regularly going in to university created a stable base that I am now in the process of shifting and rediscovering in my new role as a qualified psychologist. Whilst being qualified feels like a big step up, I feel I am discovering what I enjoy about my work and developing expertise in a specific area. I also appreciate being able to have a nine to five job, where I can go home at the end of the day and not worry about completing assignments!

When applying for qualified posts, I was surprised to find that the jobs were not as competitive as pre-qualification posts such as assistant psychologist and research assistant roles. This was a welcome relief. I had two interviews, and my current job was the second interview I attended.

Why did you decide to train as a clinical psychologist?

In all honesty, my motivation for wanting to become a clinical psychologist is the typical clichéd 'I wanted to help people' spiel! I do believe my life experiences have shaped my desire and motivation for becoming a psychologist. I am from an immigrant family, and faced many struggles growing up. I also have a younger brother with a learning disability. I am fascinated by people's ability to soldier through adversity, and the incredible amount of resilience people have in dealing with difficult life events. It is a combination of my personal struggles along with a fascination with 'struggles' that ultimately lead me to become a clinical psychologist.

What are your experiences of diversity in the profession?

Throughout my entire career, prior to qualification, during training and post-qualification, I have been the only Muslim, South Asian woman in the Psychology Team, with one exception. I am aware that my journey is very different to that of others. I have had a different type of struggle compared to some of my colleagues. It has pushed me to try harder to make sure that there is representation within the field. I have generally found colleagues have been open and accepting of me, curious about differences and respectful on the whole. It sometimes has put me in an odd position, where I want to encourage discussion relating to diversity, not just limited to race and religion, but I am acutely aware of it not becoming a tokenistic gesture or for me to become the sole representative of diversity, as I firmly believe diversity is everyone's responsibility. The most helpful conversations have been when people do not act or speak based on assumptions, and are curious and open minded, and willing to have these conversations.

In my clinical work, my race and religion has come up as an issue with some clients. Most are able to put aside any ideas, reservations and prejudices they may hold, allowing us to engage in meaningful therapeutic work. There have been a few odd occasions where that hasn't been possible. In these types of situations, I have valued when supervisors and colleagues have been empathic and understanding, whilst helping me to formulate the difficulties from multiple perspectives.

If you could give one piece of advice to someone about to pursue a career in clinical psychology, what would it be?

Maintain interests outside of clinical psychology that give you meaning and purpose in life, this will ultimately help you through some of the more difficult times on training. Balance is key; don't become complacent, always be open to new experiences and opportunities, but also learn to say no if things are getting on top of you in order to look after yourself.

What are your interests outside clinical psychology?

My friends are very important in my life. I always make sure to make time to see them, whether it's going out to see a show, be it a musical, play, opera, ballet or spoken word, having a meal, seeing an exhibition or just sitting and chatting for hours. I try to be open to new experiences, so will try different things and I love learning new skills. I also try to spend quality time with my family. Whilst socialising is a large part of my life, I value having down time to myself, where I might binge watch a TV series or movies, read books or listen to music. Singing and playing my ukulele are also hobbies I enjoy, although mostly on my own!

If you weren't working as a clinical psychologist what would you be doing?

If I wasn't a clinical psychologist, I would either find a way to be involved in outreach work, charity work, or social activism. I have also always considered myself a pro at organising events, so perhaps some type of event management role if I wanted a complete change! Whatever career I would have chosen, it would most certainly have people at its core.

EMILE'S STORY

Completed by a White British male aged 37, who identifies as a Christian.

How long have you been qualified?

Five years.

What is your area of speciality?

Adult Mental Health.

Describe the current post you are working in.

The best part of my job is when I have made a significant, life-changing difference to someone it feels very satisfying and I really appreciate having the job and the skills to do so. This is even more so when what I have done that has been helpful is clear. I enjoy developing my therapeutic understanding and skills and putting them into practice. I also enjoy helping others to develop in similar ways through teaching, supervision and consultation. Unfortunately, the above do not always go smoothly or are achieved for every patient; lack of change despite best efforts can be very frustrating. Dealing with NHS and government bureaucracy and the endless rejigging of services and finances to try to save money.

How have you found being qualified so far?

I have been qualified for over five years and am pleased to report that the long journey getting here feels worthwhile! The process of applying and being interviewed for qualified jobs has thankfully been more straightforward than for doctoral courses! I continued training in Intensive Short-Term Dynamic Psychotherapy (ISTDP) within my first year of being qualified as I felt that my learning on the course was insufficient to deliver a high-quality therapy. I feel that this training, alongside good supervision; both generic and ISTDP, enabled me to gain skills and confidence much more quickly than would otherwise have been the case. Aside from job satisfaction and a decent salary, I have gained several insights about myself and others that have been useful in my personal life in establishing and maintaining healthy relationships with myself and others.

Why did you decide to train as a clinical psychologist?

I began a business studies degree at around the same time I became a Christian. I then struggled to reconcile the direct pursuit of money with my new-found faith. I quit the business course and re-evaluated my interests and my desire to do something worthwhile. I then came up with clinical psychology and I haven't regretted that since. A Christian understanding of human nature helps me to reconcile my desire to help people with the recognition that mental health problems will always be a part of our society.

What are your experiences of diversity in the profession?

I have not personally experienced any particularly difficult challenges in relation to diversity.

If you could give one piece of advice to someone about to pursue a career in clinical psychology, what would it be?

Make sure you enjoy the journey and don't become too desperate for the 'end goal'.

What are your interests outside clinical psychology?

I play various sports and exercise such as football, badminton and general fitness activities. I enjoy going to church, studying God's word and spending time with friends.

If you weren't working as a clinical psychologist what would you be doing?

This is hard to imagine but I have become very interested in the possibilities and limitations of genetics, both naturally and in scientific manipulation; so perhaps if clinical psychology didn't exist I would be a geneticist of some sort!

SUMMARY

The clinical psychologists that we spoke with were working in a wide range of services. Their day to day work is also varied and reflects the range of roles that a clinical psychologist can undertake. The clinical psychologists had a mixed experience of diversity and, as with the trainee clinical psychologists, generally felt that the profession could be more diverse. The advice was for aspiring clinical psychologists to take their time and make the most of the journey towards becoming a clinical psychologist. The clinical psychologists provided a range of information about their own personal journeys in the career. Remember the following advice for inspiration and encouragement along your own journey:

- *Despite the pressure to demonstrate that you are very capable and competent before, during and after training, do whatever you can to hold onto enough uncertainty and doubt to be able to genuinely learn from the service users and colleagues you work with.*
- *Life still goes on; therefore, it is important not to put it on hold as you pursue your career goals. Remember that all the learning experiences you have prior to beginning training are your very own valuable foundation and should not be wasted or disregarded.*
- *Carefully consider and reflect on your reasons for following this career and whether clinical psychology would be the best choice for you. Consider the impact of the current challenges to the profession and the context of the NHS. Given these, what can you realistically bring to the profession that will support its development in the current climate.*
- *Remember to relax and cut yourself some slack. The idea that you just need to be 'good enough' as a clinical psychologist and as a human being can be liberating and therefore takes off the unnecessary pressure to that only adds to stress.*
- *It is vital to have balance. It is good to be open to new experiences and opportunities, but it is equally important to learn to say no if you are taking on too much because taking good care of yourself is vital.*

NOTE

Clinical psychology courses continue to develop ways of improving diversity in the clinical psychologists that they train. The above clinical psychologists were selected because of the types of services in which they work and because they provide a diverse representation in relation to gender and ethnicity/cultural background.

4

HOW CAN I MAKE THE MOST OF MY PSYCHOLOGY DEGREE AND WORK EXPERIENCE?

If you're an undergraduate psychologist or someone considering studying psychology in the future, this section will provide you with a range of things to consider before, during and after your undergraduate degree, what might be considered as 'relevant' experience and how you can make the most of it. Though this book mainly focuses on the clinical psychology career path, there are sections of this book that are highly applicable to alternative careers. For more details on this, see Chapter 5, 'How do I prepare for applications and interviews, and take care of myself?'

ACADEMIC WORK

There are several formal qualifications which enable people to study psychology. Here we will consider the A-level qualification offered in the UK and the undergraduate degree in psychology.

Psychology A-level

For the student considering A-levels (or equivalent, e.g. Scottish Advanced Highers) with a view to pursuing a career in Mental Health, Psychology A-level and/or other science based-subjects would be useful to choose. However, an A-level in Psychology is not a requirement to study psychology at university and some people would believe that the content of Psychology A-level studies does not prepare you adequately for study at degree level. If you do study the subject at A-level, you will cover key psychological research studies and get an overview of different theories in psychology. This provides a foundation for your knowledge as some of these ideas will likely feature in your undergraduate degree in much more detail. It would also be useful at this stage to consider which part of psychology you find the most interesting.

Whilst you're studying, it may be useful to gain experience through volunteering in schools, summer camps or community projects, both in the UK and abroad. In these settings, you would likely come across opportunities to provide mentorship and support to others; this will give you key experience in working with other people. Through these types of programmes, you can also develop increased self-confidence and leadership skills. You will often come across a diverse range of people and learn about different life circumstances and cultures to what you have been used to throughout your school years. Visit www.gapyear.com/volunteering/summer to find out more about a range of volunteering and leadership programmes that may provide you with varied learning opportunities before you embark on further studies in psychology. Further information about clinical psychology and careers in Mental Health is considered in Chapter 6.

Psychology BSc or conversion course

Once you have decided that you would like to consider a career in clinical psychology, you would then pursue a Bachelor's Degree in Psychology or, if you already have a degree in a different subject, you can complete a conversion course. To go on to study clinical psychology, your undergraduate psychology degree must allow for Graduate Basis for Chartered Membership (GBC). However, not all psychology programmes will enable GBC, so it is important to contact the course staff or the BPS, for more information on how GBC can be achieved. Alternatively, you can check this information online.

When it comes to submitting your application, considered in Chapter 5, you will be required to show evidence of your academic ability and work experience. A previous supervisor once said that when undergraduates would contact him asking for experience within his service, he would suggest to them that the best thing they can do is work towards getting the best grades possible in their degree. During your undergraduate degree, the focus should be on balancing your course work, exam preparation and your third-year dissertation as you are required to obtain a 2:1 or first-class degree. You may wish to volunteer within a relevant service if you are able to balance this with your academic work, however there is plenty of time to gain experience once you have completed your degree. It may be more practical to volunteer during your summer breaks from university and some examples of relevant volunteer placements can be found in the resources section at the back of this guide. Some courses also have an option for undergraduate students to undertake a 'year in industry' between their second and final year of the course. A number of these placements in Clinical Psychology Services are not funded. However, if this is a financially viable option it can provide an excellent opportunity to gain experience of working in the profession.

An undergraduate psychology degree provides you with the foundation for all potential careers that are psychology related and many that are not as it provides you with a broad range of skills applicable to several careers. There is an emphasis on psychology as a science throughout the course which enables you to develop your skills in research and critical appraisal, amongst other things. Your undergraduate teaching also provides you with skills, theories and approaches to understanding research that you will develop throughout your career as a clinical psychologist. Fundamentally, clinical psychologists apply psychological theory to clinical practice. For example, if a clinical psychologist were to practice Cognitive Behaviour Therapy (CBT) with a client, they would be required to understand Cognitive Theory, Behaviourism and how these ideas were integrated in the development of CBT. You will also be required to understand the research evidence which supports the use of that therapy with a particular patient group.

Whenever possible, consider opportunities to share your work. This might include presenting at conferences which may be local, regional, national or international and working towards publication with your supervisor, if possible. This helps you to develop your skills in communicating the findings of your work in different ways to a variety of audiences. Clear, consistent communication skills are essential for clinical psychology training. Although, presenting at conferences and publishing your work are not a pre-requisite for training, it will help you with the application process and to better understand your research interests and strengths. It will also help you to improve your communication skills which are very important when working as a clinical psychologist.

WORK EXPERIENCE

In order to gain a place on the Doctorate in Clinical Psychology, most courses will require you to demonstrate that you have at least one year of clinical and/or research experience in addition to the academic qualifications that you achieve. Most aspiring clinical psychologists will have applied for a variety of jobs in Clinical settings in order to develop their research and clinical skills. Some roles are in greater demand that others, i.e. assistant psychologist posts in the NHS tend to have greater number of applications and are challenging to obtain. For those with little or no clinical/research experience, voluntary work and other types of non-graduate clinical posts may be helpful in developing your experience.

There are a variety of roles that would be considered relevant experience to prepare you for training. If you undertake more than one post, you may find it beneficial to work with different clinical populations, e.g. work with children and adolescents, then working with older adults. However, this can be challenging within NHS settings, particularly when the options can be limited and the demand for those jobs is high. As a result, it is most important that you can reflect on your experiences and show what you have learnt as a result of these. This is considered in greater detail in Chapter 5 in relation to applications and clinical interviews. You should treat each clinical or research experience as an opportunity to prepare yourself for clinical psychology training and develop your skills as a clinical psychologist. As we considered in Chapter 1, some key competencies for clinical psychologists include assessment, formulation, intervention, research and evaluation, communication, leadership, supervision, teaching and personal and professional development. You can use these as a framework for how you can develop your work experience in different ways.

As discussed in Chapter 1, clinical psychologists can also work in a variety of ways within a range of services. They will work in Multi-Disciplinary Teams and may have regular contact with other agencies and organisations such as local charities, Social Services and schools. Clinical psychologists are also involved in work outside of the therapy room. For instance, they can also support with adjustment to devastating life events such as diagnosis of serious medical conditions and adjusting to physical disability. Clinical psychologists can also use their expertise to support and advise individuals or teams that care for vulnerable people who are in complex environments. As you begin to gain experience, consider what might enable you to develop your skills and consider how your experiences might prepare you for the above work.

What trainee clinical psychologists had to say!

The trainee clinical psychologists who completed the survey summarised the type of work experience they undertook prior to training. An overview of this is below.

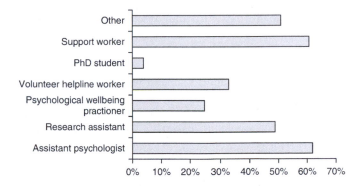

Figure 4.1 Types of work experiences undertaken by trainee clinical psychologists prior to gaining a place on doctoral programmes.

SPECIFIC ROLES

To give you a sense of what type of roles are available and what the roles requires, five specific examples are presented below. These examples are based on experiences of people who have been employed in the role, job descriptions and personal specifications. The descriptions include details about the qualifications required, skills, rewards, challenges and how to make the most of the opportunities. Although there was not scope to cover every role, many of the ideas outlined in this section may apply more broadly across different job roles and services.

These roles are for: a volunteer in a mental health charity; a support worker in a service where people have a learning disability; an assistant psychologist working with children with physical health conditions; a psychological wellbeing practitioner (PWP) working with adults who are distressed; and a research assistant involved in evaluating the effectiveness of a therapeutic approach.

Volunteer in a mental health charity

Qualifications: none required

Top five skills: understanding confidentiality requirements, good listening skills, warm, empathic, committed.

Previous experience needed? In most cases, none.

What does it involve? Providing empathic and compassionate emotional support to individuals experiencing psychological distress. You may be involved in running local social groups for people who have had experiences of mental health difficulties or provide them with practical support within their community, such as a Befriending Service.

What are the rewards of this role? Becoming a volunteer within a mental health charity can be a valuable and rewarding experience. The role provides the opportunity to learn about and understand 'honest' perspectives and individual experiences in an environment that is usually more informal than conventional Mental Health Services. Depending on the charity and its aims, you will usually be able to access good quality training in how to communicate with someone in distress, e.g. if working on a helpline. The skills acquired can include active and empathic listening which is highly valuable in any role within clinical psychology. As a volunteer, you are likely to be both challenged and inspired by people's stories. You may find that the work will lead to your own personal development and awareness of inequalities across different demographic groups. This may occur as you continue to learn from the experiences of people who may have had difficult life events and limited opportunities which have impacted on their emotional wellbeing.

Potential challenges: giving your time 'for free' is not possible for everyone and some people will require paid employment. At times, the commitment required by a volunteer organisation can come into conflict with your own work schedule, e.g. if you are asked to volunteer in the day time, when you would ordinarily be expected at a paid job elsewhere. You may also be tempted to test out the psychological and therapeutic skills you already have. However, normally, you are only permitted to use the specific skills you have been trained to use by the volunteer organisation. It is also common to send emails to a variety of organisations with your interest to volunteer or 'shadow a psychologist' and have your request declined or not get any response.

Making the most of it: despite some of the challenges outlined, it can be possible to negotiate a commitment schedule that works for you, so that you can get the best out of the time you give. There can be a lot of potential to maximise the value that can be added to a volunteering role and you could think about asking how else you can help to support the charity with the time and skill set you already have. You could suggest collecting some useful data and information for the service's development. If you have studied psychology, statistics, marketing, business (or similar) you could take the opportunity to develop questionnaires which would help the organisation gather useful data. You can then use the information you gather in a meaningful way using both qualitative methods that involve interviews or comments, and quantitative methods which may assess ratings about preferences. You could also suggest helping to develop/ update posters and leaflets or co-write an article with a service user in a local mental health newsletter. If you wanted, you could aim to volunteer in hospitals and other specialist settings that may place you in direct contact with clinical psychologists. It may be worth sending a few emails with your CV or a covering letter, stating your interest and what you feel you could offer or add to the service.

Remember: it is important that you are aware of the different ways that you can keep yourself safe if you are working alone with service users through Befriending Services for example, whereby you usually work with someone in their home or community. Ensure that you maintain your boundaries as much as possible. When we work in situations where we want to help, we can sometimes feel that we have to go 'above and beyond' our role to be useful. This can take its toll on you and can potentially be unsafe, so it is important to maintain balance and to seek support whenever possible. Always find out the policy about how to deal with inappropriate or unsafe behaviour and how report something serious that could put someone at risk. You should also be aware of who to approach for your own emotional support as the work undertaken by volunteers can potentially be overwhelming or stressful at times.

If you have completed your degree in psychology, you can access voluntary posts as an honorary assistant psychologist or honorary research assistant. This means you will be doing the same role as an assistant psychologist or research assistant but the work will be unpaid. This work can also be undertaken part-time whilst you work in a paid role elsewhere to broaden your work experience. This type of employment favours those with alternative methods of income and may not be possible for all potential trainee clinical psychologists.

How to access these roles:

There are a wide range of charities that will accept volunteers. The Appendix includes a summary of some charities where you might be able to find volunteer opportunities.

You can also access volunteer opportunities within specific services where clinical psychologists might be involved (e.g. NHS services, Private Health Services, schools/universities, community projects or initiatives run by non-profit organisations).

SUPPORT WORKER OR HEALTHCARE ASSISTANT

Qualifications: none needed

Top five skills: good communication, good team player, flexible, compassionate, creative.

Annual salary: approximately £12,000–£19,000

Previous experience needed? Sometimes, but not always. For example, previous voluntary or personal experience can be beneficial.

What does it involve? A support worker is involved in the direct care of vulnerable individuals depending on their level of need or disability. Support workers will usually report to a senior support worker, qualified nurse or service manager. They work according to agreed care or support plans for the individuals they support. For example, a support plan could include agreed strategies to manage challenging behaviour displayed by an individual within specific contexts, e.g. how to support someone who becomes anxious and overwhelmed in crowded places.

Rewards: becoming a support worker gives you direct 'hands on' clinical experience with service users. You will be involved in supporting individuals to make choices about how they would like to live their lives and contribute to their community. The organisation you work for will offer a package of training courses that increase your knowledge and skills, e.g. skills in use of specialist communication tools and managing behaviour that is challenging. In this role, you will be able to form relationships with service users and also possibly their friends and/or family members and care/therapy staff members, e.g. nurses, occupational therapists. The learning from your psychology studies about learning theories, brain and cognitive development will help you to understand the complex challenges that service users in the example above may present with.

Potential challenges: working conditions can sometimes be demanding if service users present with behaviours that challenge others and their own safety. It is important to ensure that your training in managing such situations is up to date and you can access support when it is needed. Depending on how well-staffed the team is, the role can involve long shifts with limited time to spend with service users who benefit from meaningful interactions. With any role, difficult staff team dynamics and conflict can arise. Therefore, it is essential to speak to the shift leader or manager if you have concerns. Regular one-to-one meetings with your senior colleagues may be less common in this role, so you may have to rely on informal 'check ins' with senior staff to discuss issues you want to raise. Also note that shift work patterns often involve very early starts, night shifts and weekend working.

Making the most of it: remember being a support worker presents you with the opportunity to spend a lot of time learning about and understanding the individual needs of each service user. Within your team, take opportunities to notice and share anything that is important to the people you are working with so that other staff members are encouraged to take a more individualised approach to the person. Try and get involved in the process of developing care/support plans or individualised guidelines for service users, also remembering to include their input where possible. If there is a clinical psychologist/behavioural therapist working in the service, if you can, try and meet with them for a chat and ask them if there are any ways that you can provide them with support. If you have assisted them substantially, it would be worthwhile asking if they would provide a reference for your future employment.

Remember: while support work offers important clinical experience, it can be emotionally and physically demanding. Try and make sure you speak to someone, e.g. senior colleague or manager, if you find something challenging or if you are experiencing stress as a result of aspects of the role or more generally. Even though it can feel uncomfortable, try to be honest about how you are feeling and take good care of yourself between shifts!

How to access these roles:

A variety of support worker posts are listed on www.jobs.nhs.uk. You can also access through Care and Social Care Services that exist outside of NHS services: careers.careuk.com; www.socialcare.co.uk.

Other general job websites, i.e. www.indeed.co.uk, will advertise support worker roles. Some of these roles may even involve supporting an individual person within their family home on a full-time basis.

ASSISTANT PSYCHOLOGIST

Qualifications: Bachelor's Degree in Psychology or a Conversion Master's Degree accredited by the British Psychological Society.

Top five skills: enthusiastic, good interpersonal skills, show initiative, good time management, empathic.

Starting annual salary: approximately, £18,000–£25,000

Previous experience needed? Often these roles will require relevant or related clinical experience, e.g. support work with the client group, research and volunteer experience are all helpful.

What does it involve? Assistant psychologists provide a clinical service under the direction and supervision of a qualified clinical psychologist who has the ultimate responsibility for the work carried out. For example, working with children and young people who have a physical health condition, an assistant psychologist could be involved in interviewing families and assessing children using psychological tools and instruments. They can also carry out specific psychological interventions for targeted difficulties, e.g. support to overcome needle phobia for young people requiring regular injections.

Rewards: this post is usually supervised by a qualified clinical psychologist who might meet with you for an hour, a couple times per month, to discuss your work, progress and development (guidelines on the supervision requirements for assistant psychologists are produced by the BPS). You will most likely be able to apply psychological theories you studied during your undergraduate degree. In the above example, you may need to think about how developmental, social/family factors and physical difficulties interact to impact on emotional distress.

In this role, or similar, you may have the opportunity to learn how to help people using therapeutic approaches that clinical psychologists regularly apply. Assistant psychologists often use psychometric tools, which are questionnaires measuring different aspects of wellbeing, and may conduct assessments to determine the impact of changes in the brain using neuropsychological tests under supervision of a qualified psychologist. You may work in a team that consists of other professionals who may enrich your knowledge and experience such as: psychiatrists, nurses, psychotherapists, art, play and music therapists.

Potential challenges: assistant psychologist posts are high in demand, but supply is limited so it may take longer to secure a position compared with other roles. In addition, you may want to consider relocating to another region of the country or travel further to open up more options for you. Some posts are offered on a fixed-term basis of six months to one year which means that you may need to look for another job well before your contract ends. Some assistant psychologist jobs may involve more administration duties than clinical experience, if any, so it is important to read the job description thoroughly and ask about the type and amount of clinical experience at interview or when you have been made an offer. Working with other assistant psychologists can feel competitive or anxiety provoking, particularly around the time of applying or interviewing for clinical psychology training courses. Make sure you seek support when you need it; this might be from your supervisor, or from your friends and family.

Making the most of it: psychology graduates working as an assistant psychologist can bring a broad range of skills to a service such as research and clinical skills. It is worth noting that some people working as an assistant psychologist may feel that they have to undertake more administration-based tasks initially before they are able to get involved in clinical or research work. When opportunities arise, ask to get involved in conducting a piece of service-related research if you can. This can involve collecting interview or survey data based on user experiences of the service; stress or stressors in the workplace for staff; looking at the factors related to non-attendance or non-compliance to treatment or therapy; analysing data on non-attendance of appointments. These findings can be presented to the team or even be submitted for publication in the *Clinical Psychology Forum*, a DCP magazine.

You could also speak to your supervisor about visiting other services or organisations that your workplace has a relationship with and see whether you could 'shadow' another professionals' work to broaden your learning. It might also be beneficial to get involved in staff training in psychological approaches or presenting a case study, that was successful or unsuccessful, for both learning and teaching purposes. You can also make the most of your clinical psychologist supervisor's own experience and ask them to look over your clinical psychology doctorate application form, as well as supporting you with preparing for interviews.

Remember: as an assistant psychologist, it is important that you are aware that your supervisor is accountable for your clinical work. You should receive regular supervision and the frequency and duration should be agreed at the start of the job role. Though it may feel uncomfortable, let your supervisor know when you become aware that you have made a mistake and when you feel stressed or overwhelmed by the work. It's important to be aware of your strengths and weaknesses and ask for help and support when the need arises. Your supervisors can then assist you in developing further and help with your personal and professional growth.

How to access the roles:

A variety of assistant psychologist posts are usually advertised on www.jobs.nhs.uk. Try and use a variety of search terms when searching for positions, such as 'assistant psychologist', 'assistant clinical psychologist', 'psychology assistant', 'assistant clinical neuropsychologist', 'psychological assistant' and 'research assistant psychologist'.

The BPS *Psychologist* magazine and standard recruitment websites also list assistant psychologist roles, some of which are not based within the NHS. There are some occasions where support workers are encouraged to apply for newly created assistant psychologist positions within the same service. Therefore, it is worth speaking to the psychologists within the service to find out more about the role, as well as the selection process and criteria.

PSYCHOLOGICAL WELLBEING PRACTITIONER (PWP) WORKING WITH ADULT MENTAL HEALTH PROBLEMS

Qualifications: you will need to hold at least a Bachelor's Degree in, e.g. Nursing, Psychology, Occupational Therapy, Social Work.

Top five skills: motivated, show initiative, organised, empathic, good time management skills.

Starting annual salary: trainee PWP £18,000 and qualified PWP £21,000.

Previous experience needed? Experience and understanding of work with people with mental health difficulties.

What does it involve? PWPs work within the Improving Access to Psychological Therapies (IAPT) Wellbeing Services provided by the NHS. They provide psychological interventions for people who have a variety of presentations, which include anxiety and depression, using CBT, using a manual to guide the therapy.

Rewards: training to become a PWP is commissioned specifically in local universities. The 12-month training course provides you with one day per week of teaching and four days of practical experience and is paid. Becoming a psychological wellbeing practitioner offers you a Postgraduate Certificate qualification and is a career path all on its own with scope for further development of clinical skills in Cognitive Behavioural Therapy within the same clinical group. Some PWP's gain enough experience to then go on to train as high-intensity cognitive behavioural therapists, who can work in the private sector with accredited qualifications. This post also offers more job security with permanent contracts compared to many assistant posts which often offer more fixed term employment, e.g. six months or one-year fixed term. You will benefit from a great deal of clinical experience as PWPs come into contact with a high volume of clients due to the short-term nature of interventions as usually only six sessions of therapy are offered per client. You may also get the opportunity to run short term group therapy sessions.

Potential challenges: the high caseloads that PWP's often manage can restrict the amount and quality of formulation and reflection, and clinical supervision can be limited due to the busy and pressured environment. PWP's work from one dominant model of Cognitive Behavioural Therapy and can therefore limit your exposure to broader models and theories that many clinical psychologists would ordinarily draw from in their work. Clients may present with more complex social and psychological problems than the PWP training prepares you for and it is important to discuss these issues regularly and seek support from your supervisor and colleagues.

Making the most of it: even though the post can be very busy, try and take note of a few clients that have interested or challenged you and practice thinking about the work from different perspectives using different psychological theories or models. Some people keep a reflective diary to document a record of their experience. This will be useful if you change jobs or attend clinical psychology course interviews, as it demonstrates that you can think outside of a cognitive behavioural formulation. Try and get together with other PWPs and psychological therapists in your workplace think jointly about specific cases that are particularly challenging to work with. You can then formulate ways in which to get through obstacles in therapy, drawing on the knowledge and experience of your colleagues.

Remember: the high caseload can put a lot of pressure on PWPs, so remember to take care of yourself and if you are feeling overwhelmed, please seek support. Being organised, prioritising and planning ahead are important skills that should be cultivated as you develop within this role. These abilities will also be important when embarking on clinical training which involves multiple components such as managing workload on placement, research and academic demands.

How to access these roles:

You can access PWP job roles on www.jobs.nhs.uk as well as charities such as www.mind.org.uk, www.turning-point.co.uk, www.rethink.org. You can also find out more about the role and the IAPT scheme here: www.iapt.nhs.uk.

RESEARCH ASSISTANT

Qualifications: Bachelor's Degree (usually BSc; in some posts, an MSc is also required).

Top five skills: organised, thorough, takes initiative, works well in a team, good communication skills.

Annual salary: approximately £19,000–£26,000.

Previous experience needed? Sometimes. It would be particularly beneficial if you have experience working in other Clinical or Research settings. Alternatively, a relevant research dissertation from your studies or other research experience may also be useful. You may be able to gain experience working with a lecturer on their research at university. It is worth asking what opportunities may be available when you're an undergraduate as well as seeking postgraduate experience.

What does it involve? The role involves recruiting participants to take part in the research study, collecting and analysing data from interviews, focus groups and questionnaires that have been administered. A research assistant also contributes to preparing the research data collected for presentation at conferences or publication in psychology journals.

Rewards: a research assistant has the opportunity to take part in supporting the development of research evidence that may go on to influence the way in which clinical psychologists and related professions work. There are opportunities to work within a variety of settings including collecting research data in care homes, day centres, hospital settings and with a variety of relevant individuals involved, i.e. nurses, psychiatrists, family members and direct work with clients. There may be a variety of opportunities to attend events that will enhance your learning, such as special interest group meetings and research conferences where alternative psychological concepts and issues are presented. Developing these research skills will be a good way of preparing yourself for research activities undertaken on the clinical psychology training course. This will enable you to conduct clinical research, evaluate services and interventions. Depending on your input in the writing and editing of a research paper, there will also be opportunities for you to be named on the journal publication, which enhances your CV.

Potential challenges: though research activities can be highly rewarding, the clinical experience they offer can be limited if the role is mainly administrative. If this is the case, it will primarily involve conducting literature searches and writing academic articles, amongst other things. Such a role may be a useful starting point in order to later gain a more psychologically relevant and client facing research role. At times research activities are likely to span over several years, so you may not have the time or opportunity to see the entire research process through to the end. Some posts are not supervised by clinical psychologists and therefore supervision is often task focussed, rather than reflective supervision which centres on the discussion of therapeutic work.

Making the most of it: it is important to be proactive. If you find that you have some time to dedicate to completing a detailed literature search, you can ask your supervisor if you could write up a literature review with a view to having this published. Once you have agreed and committed to doing this, it is possible to continue working on the publication once you have left the post. It might be worth asking if you could join or shadow some of the clinical work being conducted or led by clinical psychologists within the services you come across during your time as a research assistant. Be prepared to search proactively for any events that may be related to the area of research you are working in, such as those being run by relevant charities. By making contact with such organisations you will be showing initiative and increasing the 'reach' of clinical research to the wider communities who can contribute to the development of research activities from their lived experiences. Keeping a research log or diary can help you with the process of reflecting on your experiences as well as keeping a track of your progress and future goals.

Remember: research takes time and there are many steps and obstacles along the way to making the project happen. Try to develop positive relationships with your colleagues so that you can derive support from them, when things are more challenging. The research environment can be fast paced and pressured, so ensure that you take care of yourself, ask for help when needed and speak to your supervisor if the workload feels unmanageable at any point.

How to access these roles:

Research assistant jobs can be found on www.jobs.nhs.uk or www.jobs.ac.uk. Some mental health charities will advertise research assistant roles, so it may be worth searching for vacancies of their websites (see above in the Volunteer section for examples).

Have a go!

Start your own reflective journal. Get a notepad and jot down some of your experiences. This approach can help you to reflect on any work and/or research experience that you might have and may include some of the roles considered above.

- What did you do in that role?
- What did you enjoy?
- What did you learn?
- What skills did you develop?
- If you were doing the same thing again, what would you do differently?

What trainee clinical psychologists had to say!

The preceding job roles discussed are by no means an exhaustive list. They are intended to illustrate examples of the rewards and challenges of common roles as well as showing how to make the most of a select few posts. Many people have a variety of job titles and demonstrate more unconventional routes to clinical training. During our journeys within clinical psychology, we met people who came from different careers that included law, sports, work in human resources, carpet sales and even an experienced melon picker! These distinct roles are also likely to grab the attention and intrigue of future job or course selectors. From the trainees that completed our questionnaire the following were some of the 'other' relevant job roles they undertook:

- victim support volunteer;
- outreach worker;
- IAPT employment support coordinator;
- trainee/graduate mental health worker;
- senior PWP lecturer;
- volunteer mentor in learning disabilities;
- behaviour support worker;

- honorary assistant psychologist;
- honorary research assistant;
- befriender;
- camp counsellor/play leader;
- teaching assistant;
- healthcare assistant;
- care assistant manager;
- psychiatrist's assistant;
- programmes officer;
- research team coordinator;
- clinical studies officer;
- trainee clinical associate in applied psychology;
- learning assistant for children with special needs;
- family worker;
- child and adolescent therapist;
- social worker;
- key worker in a probation hostel for sex offenders;
- community development worker;
- smoking cessation worker.

The responses above show that there are a different range of relevant work experiences that people can bring to clinical psychology training.

OTHER CONSIDERATIONS WHEN MAKING THE MOST OF YOUR EXPERIENCE

Continual professional development (CPD)

CPD is how people invest and develop their skills and knowledge over time. As you embark on the path to become a budding clinical psychologist, it is important to pursue as many learning opportunities as you can. Not only will they help you to write attractive job applications and answer job interview questions well, they also expand your capacity to reflect and critically analyse current research and clinical practices.

Networking

Networking in a professional context involves developing and nurturing relationships with your colleagues, both where you work and within other associated organisations. Attending conferences such as those organised by the BPS DCP pre-qualification group would be useful and joining local assistant psychologist or pre-training groups would also help you to network with your peers and have a support network consisting of like-minded people. Most of these can be accessed through an online search or through talking to other assistant psychologists in your geographical area.

Salary expectations

You may want to consider aiming to gain a post that affords you both good quality work experience and offers a salary that works for you as you pursue this career. Pay varies according to the role and your location in the UK. For example, pay will usually be higher within larger cities/locations which have greater living costs (e.g. inner London). For more information about pay scales in the NHS visit: www.nhsemployers.org/your-workforce/pay-and-reward/agenda-for-change/pay-scales.

Salaries are usually lower when embarking on the journey towards being a clinical psychologist, however, once qualified clinical psychologists are generally paid well in the context of other health professionals. The starting salary of a newly qualified clinical psychologist is £31,383 outside of London. However, it is important to bear in mind that the pressures of Health Services discussed earlier means that the number of high paid leadership roles have been reduced and the earning potential of clinical psychologists working in the NHS has reduced.

Improve your job applications

Some people may wonder why they keep getting rejections or not hearing anything at all from jobs that they are applying for. The following may be helpful, and we discuss more information about writing good applications and preparing for interview in Chapter 5:

Before applying:

- Make sure you meet the minimum requirements for the job role as a variety of relevant jobs will require a completed degree with a minimum 2:1 classification, as well as relevant experience.
- Ensure you understand the role as much as possible and that you have read the job description.

When completing the application:

- Use examples from your work that show that you meet both the essential and desirable criteria found in the person specification. Make it clear why you are applying for this job in particular.
- Talk about why you as a person and your experience would be suited to that specific role, e.g. how does your research role looking at the impact of social support on parenting skills relate to a new assistant psychologist role working with families of children with autism?
- Don't only list your work experiences and skills but show your capacity to reflect on what you learnt from them.
- Ask for another person, preferably someone who is in a similar or senior position in their profession, to look over your application form. They can comment on the way you have written your application and also correct common spelling and grammatical mistakes.

After the interview:

- Try and call the service after not hearing back from them. The interviewers may not offer any feedback on your application at all, but it is possible that they may take the time to give you helpful feedback.

Improve your interview skills

Some people may wonder why they are being invited to interviews but do not subsequently receive a job offer. If this is the case, the following may be helpful in improving your interview techniques:

- Read and familiarise yourself with the main public policies relating to working within the clinical group or project you are hoping to work with.
- It may be worth googling your interviewers to find out whether they have done any work research that you can mention in your answers.
- Think about the role and imagine what it might be like to work within the service and clinical group so that your answers feel more natural when you are given scenarios.
- Though you might feel very nervous, try to manage your anxiety, speak with clarity and project compassion and enthusiasm.
- Take your time to answer questions and ask the interviewer to repeat the question if needed.
- Use examples from your work/personal experiences or reading where relevant.
- Practice interviews with trusted colleagues, family or friends.
- Always seek feedback following unsuccessful interviews so that you can learn about how you can improve in the future.

In Chapter 5, we expand upon how to improve your interview skills in preparation for the clinical psychology training course. The information presented there will be helpful in developing your interview skills for any job for which you decide to apply.

What trainee clinical psychologists had to say!

The trainee clinical psychologists described what they found useful when gaining relevant experience. The following quotes will help you to improve your understanding of how they made the most of their experiences. The comments relate to:

- The value of getting a wide range of work experience:

  'Clinical experience within a range of different settings (Primary Care, Secondary Care, Multi-Disciplinary Teams).'

  'I learned that working in Mental Health should not just be about get onto the course but experience which genuinely makes you more robust and prepared for training.'

- Developing confidence:

  'My most recent role (not an assistant psychologist post) allowed me to integrate into a Community Mental Health Team, manage my own caseload, and be autonomous in deciding what was best for my clients. This led to me familiarising myself with the National Institute for Clinical Excellence (NICE) guidelines and completing various training programmes to upskill. This gave me the confidence in my clinical skills and pushed me to apply.'

- Feeling prepared to apply to and begin the course:

  'It was through building up my own professional identity in psychology/mental health work that I then felt in the best place to embark on training. If you don't truly understand the nature of the NHS, the client work, the daily challenges of the work you might be underprepared.'

- Being well supported:

  'Having excellent supervisors early on in my career was pivotal in teaching me how to reflect on my skills, what I brought to a session with a client and how I could develop professionally in terms of attending training and conferences.'

- Seeking good advice:

  'Advice from qualified psychologists and trainees has been invaluable! It's really important to understand the current challenges both in trying to get onto training and getting through it once you are on.'

- Being proactive and taking the initiative to seek out relevant experience:

  'I found my assistant jobs to be quite specialised (sometimes with little clinically relevant experience) so I made it my business to ask around to see if there was anything I could help with or observe to make sure I was getting the best out of my jobs.'

- Thinking critically and reflecting on your work:

  'Developing the ability to take feedback and use it wisely to advance my experiences was good. I was able to persuade other professionals to give me opportunities to work with clinical psychologists to understand what the field entailed.'

  'Being able to reflect on my practice . . . helped me to be able to better consider alternative perspectives and also to think about the importance of self-care as a psychologist who has to hold and manage other people's distress.'

- Seeing the rewards and the usefulness of different roles that are available:

  'One of my voluntary assistant psychologist posts. I had two; one of which was not very helpful but the other which provided me with great direct client experience under supervision of a clinical psychologist.'

  'Despite the many downsides, my time as a health care assistant was extremely useful as I was able to prove to

*myself that I am emotionally resilient enough to cope with
other people's distress, and am able to keep a cool head
when someone needs me to.'*

*'Working in IAPT helped me gain lots of clinical experience
and working directly with psychologists.'*

SUMMARY

There are a range of clinical and research opportunities which
will enable you to develop your skills and prepare you for your
training as a clinical psychologist. These include volunteering,
employment as a support worker, an assistant psychologist, a
psychological wellbeing practitioner and a research assistant.
There are a range of other roles which will also count as a relevant experience when applying to train as a clinical psychologist
as they will enable you to develop the required skills and competencies. It is most important to demonstrate what you have
learnt from your experience rather than only describing what
you did. Most people apply for multiple roles when pursuing a
career as a clinical psychologist and it is important to continue
to improve your applications and develop your skills at interview
and throughout the process.

At undergraduate level, it is important to focus on your academic work as a priority. However, if you can balance this and
spend time volunteering then it can help you gain relevant experience and think about whether or not you would like to work as
a clinical psychologist. Make the most of your learning; it will
all be useful in a career in which you are continually developing
your knowledge. Your undergraduate studies form the foundation of your theoretical understanding and critical appraisal skills
and they will be valuable to you in the future. Take opportunities to distribute the findings from your work; teach others about
what you've found and work towards publication, if possible.

5

HOW DO I PREPARE FOR APPLICATIONS AND INTERVIEWS, AND TAKE CARE OF MYSELF?

Once you have completed your undergraduate degree, gained relevant experience and feel that clinical psychology is the profession for you, this chapter of the book provides the guidance for completing the doctorate application and preparing for the course interviews. As in previous chapters, we include a mix of information about the process primarily from the Clearing House website, the authors' personal experiences and advice from people who have been through the process. Before we consider the questions that you have to answer on the application form, it is first worth considering the following statement:

'IF YOU WANT TO BE A CLINICAL PSYCHOLOGIST THEN YOU NEED TO KNOW WHY'

Some people are excited by the idea of being part of a profession that is relatively young (particularly when compared to medicine) and that comes with all sorts of potential for development. Clinical psychology also provides opportunity to work in a variety of ways, i.e. therapist, neuropsychologist, researcher, advocate, manager, consultant, leader, supervisor, etc.

Clinical psychology trainees often have a variety of personal and professional reasons for choosing to work in the profession. Think about what these are for you and what has led you here. For example, Steve grew up around people who were distressed and noticed they were mostly given medication to help. This didn't seem logical to him and understanding psychology and the clinical application of psychology gave him ways to better understand and talk about this. Having made a huge cultural transition after moving from Zimbabwe to the UK at the age of 12, Amanda experienced the stress and challenges of adjusting to a new social environment, with new rules and pressures. This personal experience increased her interest in understanding the process of adjusting to change. In addition, it motivated her to want to pursue a profession that attempts to understand human distress and the ways that it can be alleviated through the clinical and academic application of psychology.

Why is the work of a clinical psychologist valuable to you? Is there anyone you look up to who has done this kind of work and why do they inspire you? Do you have any personal experiences that have drawn you to the work that a clinical psychologist may undertake? It may be that you have had positive or negative experiences of the Mental Health system as an employee or service user and might want to make a difference.

Why have *you* come down this path towards becoming a clinical psychologist? What experiences have led you to this path (past and present)?

Have a go!
- Write a list of reasons why you want to be a clinical psychologist.
- Write down why this profession is important to you.
- Write down your thoughts about what you would uniquely bring to the profession.
- Write down how your personal journey has led you to this career path.

Now that you have a sense of why you want to train as a clinical psychologist, you'll be in a better position to tackle the application and interview processes.

UK APPLICATIONS

The application form for the Doctorate in Clinical Psychology in the UK is completed online via the Clearing House website (www. leeds.ac.uk/chpccp/index.html). As we mentioned earlier, there are three courses offering self-funded places (as of 2017) and two of these will accept direct applications. This is likely to change in subsequent years and it is useful to check the Clearing House website for up to date information. This website displays information relevant to course centres, applications and interviews in an accessible way. The applications are available for completion from September to November/early December each year. Over the past few years, the questions on the application forms for clinical psychology trainees have largely remained the same with requirements for respondents to be concise as the responses are limited by characters. It is very important that the applications are well written and well presented. Any errors in grammar and spelling could count against you due to the competitive nature of the course. The information required for the application form includes:

Courses that you are applying for

You have a choice of four courses that you can select. Trainee clinical psychologists will choose different courses for a variety of reasons which can depend on the course location, teaching emphasis (some courses may prefer a certain type of theoretical approach to clinical practice), the selection procedure (screening assessments and then interview or direct interview), method of evaluation (exams, coursework or both), the style of thesis (some courses require the research to be presented as a large thesis and others require smaller documents which may be easier to publish), amongst other things. A brief summary from each course is available on the Clearing House website and you can access more information on the websites of the individual courses.

A-level qualifications

This can include other relevant qualifications (Psychology A-level is not required).

University qualifications

Your psychology undergraduate or conversion degree that provides Graduate Basis for Chartered Membership (and any other university qualifications such as Master's of PhD qualification).

Relevant experience

Provide a list of all work and/or research experience that you have. There is space to record each job separately and to provide some brief points about what your responsibilities were in this role.

Relevant experience – other experience

This section can be used to explain any gaps in CV and describe time spent travelling. It can also be used to detail any other relevant information that may not fit into another section of the application but is relevant for the assessors to know when considering your application. Some people may use this section to detail CPD courses that they have attended.

In what way have your work and/or research experiences made you a better candidate for training in clinical psychology?

This is the main question in the application process and it is an opportunity for you to show what you have learnt from the work and/or research experiences you have. The emphasis here is not what you've done, but what you learnt and how these experiences make you suitable to train as a clinical psychologist.

Publications or disseminations from your work

This can be used to list publications, articles, presentations, leaflets or any other time that your work has been made available publicly. You should list your academic publications first as they're most relevant and use the American Psychological Association (APA) standards for all academic referencing. Guidance is widely available online.

What would you hope to gain from training?

Here is your opportunity to say what you hope to develop during clinical psychology training. Some people might talk about how they hope to develop their skills as a clinician or researcher.

Other information about yourself, i.e. interests outside of psychology

If you need to explain the relationship to your referees or if there are any other factors relevant in assessing your application, then you are able to provide these details here.

References

You need to provide the details of two references: usually one clinical and one academic. The references need to be a very high standard. Although they don't necessarily need to be from a certain type of professional, clinical psychologists who have been through the training process may understand the importance of these references. Some courses don't use the these at all but will ask for current employer references. A copy of the form for completing the references is available from the Clearing House or at: www.leeds.ac.uk/chpccp/SampleReferenceAcademic.pdf.

What trainee clinical psychologists had to say!

Here is some advice from trainee clinical psychologists about preparing the application form. The trainees echoed some of the points made by the trainee and clinical psychologists whom we heard from in Chapters 2 and 3. Their comments related to four key themes: *put in the ground work, make your application stand out, manage your expectations* and *maintain balance,* which are described below.

Put in the ground work

The trainee clinical psychologists said that before you complete the form, it is worth getting more information about the courses, how you can meet the core competencies of training and to consider what will help you to stand out from other applicants:

> *'Try to remember what makes you stand out from the 100s of other people applying and try to get this across.'*

> *'Speak to psychologists and trainees. If you don't know any ask friends, family or use careers networks.'*

> *'Keep a log book of your experiences, consider the core competencies for clinical psychology training. Keep examples of times when you've been challenged, used formulations effectively, had difficulties with a supervisor and how you resolved this.'*

Make your application stand out

With only 15% of applicants gaining a place on a training course each year, it is important that your application is of excellent quality. The trainee clinical psychologists said that you can do this by avoiding buzzwords, making every word court, showing your ability to reflect, your awareness of key issues in the practice of clinical psychology and how you can meet the requirements of the course:

> *'Don't use too many buzzwords/jargon. If you do use buzzwords make sure you include clear examples of your knowledge and reflections.'*

> *'Every word should count for something – no fluff!'*

> *'Write concisely, don't repeat words written in other parts of the form.'*

> *'Get someone else to read it for you.'*

> *'Reflect. Reflect. Reflect. Don't just list your experiences, reflect on them.'*

> *'Think carefully about the course approach and how your experience can fit with their needs.'*

'Show your knowledge of leadership, changing nature of psychology, the NHS and teaching of others.'

'Don't try to be the perfect candidate – be authentic, be yourself in a way that can convey your personality.'

'Get a clinical psychologist to write your references, even if they don't know you as well as someone else.'

Manage your expectations

The trainee clinical psychologists suggested that it is important to balance your expectations in relation to training, take your time before applying, reminding yourself that most people don't get on first time:

'It's just a job application, don't worry too much about getting on and enjoy and make the most of your pre-training experience. It's pretty stressful when you get on so make the most of (relatively) stress-free jobs.'

'Remember that most people don't get on to training the first time that they apply.'

Maintain balance

Due to the increased competition and sense of powerlessness that some applicants might feel, the trainee clinical psychologists recommend maintaining balance through the application process. They suggest that you can do this by giving yourself enough time, getting support from others, having other things in your life and ensuring that you 'switch off' once the form is submitted:

'Take your time with it – don't do it last minute.'

'Seek advice from a small number of people as too much advice can be hindering and sometimes conflicting.'

'Get people to have a read – at least one within and one from outside of clinical psychology.'

'Get the form close to finished then leave it for one to two weeks, come back at it with fresh eyes.'

'Make sure there is more in your life than just the application process.'

'Once your application is in, as hard as it is, forget about it.'

The above advice will help you to consider how best to approach different aspects of the form and how to think about the application process. The following section relates to how to prepare for an interview for the clinical psychology training courses.

PRE-INTERVIEW ASSESSMENTS

For a number of years, some courses have introduced a pre-interview assessment process to help select which applicants are invited for interview. These assessment sessions vary between courses and it is worth checking if the course to which you're applying requires you to complete an assessment. If they do, ask for information about what the assessment will entail and how it helps to inform the decision-making process is likely to be available on the course website. Some people find the assessment process useful and others would prefer a process where you go directly to interview. It is an individual decision and may help to inform what courses you choose to apply for.

Interviews

Once you have completed the application form, you will have a few months of waiting before you find out if you are going to be invited to an assessment or interview. During this time, as the trainees suggested above, it is important to maintain balance and try to focus on important things in your life, unrelated to the application process. More often than not, applicants receive a rejection letter, particularly on their first attempt at the application. This does not mean that you are not a suitable candidate for clinical training and with consideration of how you can continue to improve and develop, most people who persevere have a higher chance of submitting a successful application. For example, Steve applied for training four times and was not offered a place for three years before being accepted to the University of Leeds training course.

When you do receive an invitation to an interview, there is no right or wrong way to prepare. Some people take time and plan the process in advance whereas some people prefer to work under the last minute 'pressure'. Regardless of your preferred style of preparation, it is important to ensure that you consider the amount of information you need to cover and allow enough time for revision and practice interview questions. This is the best way to ensure you have an opportunity to be successful at interview.

Your practice for interviews should not only focus on specific examples of questions and how you can answer them as it will be obvious to the panel if the response is pre-prepared and you may sound less genuine. Another risk is that you may try and make their question fit with an answer that you have rehearsed, rather than answering the actual question that has been asked. In consideration of this, you should focus on themes of questions in order to consider broader topics and examples that you may wish to discuss, which will hopefully mean you will be able to answer any question. Courses will generally ask questions that will get you to think 'on the spot' as clinical psychologists are often required to demonstrate responsive thinking under pressure.

As you think about the broad topics and examples that might be relevant to interviews, follow the advice of the psychologists in relation to completing the application form, making sure to reflect. There are several ways to structure the reflective process and some models that you may wish to consider are Gibbs (1988) and Johns (1995). Generally, most models require you to reflect on what you did, why you did it, what you learnt, what you would do differently next time and how it impacted on you as a person. The broad topics to consider in preparation for the interview relate to research, current issues concerning the NHS, clinical work and personal experiences. Some courses will ask you to talk more about your knowledge and experiences giving examples, whereas others may require you to apply your knowledge to a specific scenario but not talk about your own experiences. When talking about your experiences, the STARR approach can be helpful when answering questions such as 'tell us about a time when you. . .' STARR stands for:

Situation	what is the scenario that you are describing?
Target	what did you decide to do in this situation and why?
Action	what did you do?
Result	what happened as a result of your actions or those of another person?
Reflection	following the situation, what do you think about what happened? What have you learnt? Is there anything you would do differently next time?

Research

Be prepared to talk about the research that you have been involved in. This could be your undergraduate dissertation or another audit, service evaluation or research project that you've facilitated. Considering the STARR model above, you should be able to talk about why the research was carried out (what was the background, rationale and aims), what you did (your method and reason for choosing this approach/alternative methods), how you analysed or understood the data, the key findings and the limitations from the work.

Consider the links between your research findings and how they relate to the practice of clinical psychology. You can also consider how the theory behind your research also applies to Clinical settings. It is also useful to think about how you could build on your research and develop the ideas further, demonstrating your critical and analytical thinking.

It is important to review research methodology, which is how the research was carried out, and you may recall different research methods from studying your undergraduate psychology degree. It is worth reviewing your notes, referring to a research textbook and also doing a literature search to refresh your mind on different ways of conducting research. Consider quantitative and qualitative approaches to research and think about the benefits and limitations of these methods. Be prepared to design a study to evaluate a particular approach, such as the effectiveness of a psychological intervention, during the interview. Re-familiarise yourself with research design, hypothesis-testing, group designs, statistical analysis and qualitative analysis. It can also be helpful to have read of one or two clinically relevant research papers and be able to critique them, if required.

Be prepared to show the panel what you know. It is unlikely that all of the above will be required for an interview, but if you can prepare for talking thoughtfully about clinical research, as well as research design, then there should be no big surprises during the interview.

Have a go!

Write down a summary of some research that you've been involved in:

- What was the background, rationale and aims?
- What was your method and reason for choosing this approach?
- How did you analyse the data?
- What are the key findings and limitations from the work?
- What would you do differently if starting the research again?
- How do your findings relate to practice of clinical psychology?
- Are there any ethical issues that you should consider?

Clinical work

In preparation for the clinical interview, you should be prepared to have a few cases that you can talk about in detail. Think about the people with whom you have worked or known about in the services where you've worked and consider how you can reflect on these experiences. Usually, it is good practice to be able to discuss an example of when your work went well, didn't go well or where there was a complex issue (i.e. a client you found it challenging to work with). When talking about these experiences, it is good practice to be able to describe it in a similar way to this:

> *'I was working with "X" and "X" happened. I felt "X" and I decided to do "X". Afterwards I thought "X" and felt "X". I decided to seek support or advice from my supervisor/manager/etc. If I were to face this again, I would do "X" because "X". I have learnt "X" about myself and my work through this experience.'*

The above format allows you to demonstrate how you can not only talk about your experience and describe complex clinical examples, but how you have reflected on and learnt from these. As with the research questions, you should be able to consider what the issues may be in relation to a scenario that you might be given (also known as a 'vignette').

Have a go!

Think about a case that you have worked with and write down answers to the following questions:

- Who was the person? Describe them anonymously and using only essential information – e.g. 'person in the service who was experiencing distress as a result of hearing derogatory voices', may suffice.
- What was your role?
- What happened in the work?
- What did you do?
- How did you access support?
- What did you learn?
- What would you do differently next time?
- Can you apply psychological theory to the challenge or dilemma you faced?

Current NHS and professional issues

It will be useful to familiarise yourself with the key issues, policies and changes in the NHS and the profession of clinical psychology (and have an opinion on them). As of 2018, these include the impact of privatisation and austerity on Health Care and initiatives like *Five Year Forward View* for Mental Health (Mental Health Taskforce, 2016). In January 2018, the Power Threat Meaning Framework (PTMF) was produced by a group of clinical psychologists as an alternative to psychiatric diagnosis Johnstone et al. (2018). You can find an overview and main version of this controversial document online. You can also find out more about these issues by looking at *Clinical Psychology Forum*, some of these are available for free online and you can access all versions if you are a DCP member. You can also read about them on the Department of Health (DoH) website and some issues will be discussed in mainstream media (usually in the *Guardian* and *Independent* newspapers) and on Twitter (consider following some of the leaders in the profession if you are a social media user). In most NHS teams, key issues and policies will be discussed regularly so it can be useful to talk to service managers about what policies and issues are pertinent in their service.

Have a go!

Find out about a current issue in NHS services relating to clinical psychology and then answer the following questions.

- What has created this issue?
- What factors are maintaining the issue?
- What is the impact on the people accessing the services?
- What is the impact on the teams supporting these people?
- Can you consider what might reduce the impact of the issue?

Personal experiences

This relates back to the beginning of the chapter when you considered: 'Why do you want to be a clinical psychologist?' The interview may require you to think about what has happened to you, or people you know, that may have influenced your decision to train as a clinical psychologist. Review your answer to the question at the beginning of this section and before the interview, have a clear idea of how much of your personal experiences you are prepared to disclose and how you would talk about these experiences in front of a panel of strangers.

Questions for the interviewers

Be prepared to ask questions of the interviewers. Show that you're interested in the course and finding out more about it. You might want to know more about the method of assessment, service user involvement on the course, types of placements available, what their current trainees like about the course, opportunities for peer support (particularly if you're moving to a new city), research interests of the department, etc. However, only ask genuine questions rather than something for the sake of it. Overall, it won't make a difference to the interview process.

Bringing it all together

If you have been offered an interview for clinical training, the assessors are already impressed with your application. Also, the likelihood of being offered a place at the interview stage is much higher and usually one in four to one in five interviewees are selected. It is important to relax, be yourself and show them how you can talk about your knowledge and experiences. This is easier said than done and it's okay to feel anxious and everyone else going through the interview process is likely to feel the same. Each training course has their preferences for trainees and a rejection does not reflect you personally. Most people find that they get accepted on a course that suits them and the style of questioning in some courses fits better with some people more than others. Some courses also have other interview components (group tasks, written tasks, research and clinical panels, service user panels) but you will be given more information about this when you receive your invitation letter.

We decided not to include any example questions in the book as this would be an unfair and unequal representation for courses. Also, if the questions became publicly available then the courses may be likely to change the questions and they may become quickly outdated. If you are ready to talk about your work, research and other experiences in the ways discussed above, you should then be ready to answer most of the potential questions!

What trainee clinical psychologists had to say!

Here is some advice from trainee clinical psychologists about preparing for interviews. The trainees echoed some of the points made above and their comments related to key themes about how to 'prepare yourself', 'be yourself', 'make the most of the opportunity', 'acknowledge your limits', 'manage anxiety' and 'maintain perspective'.

Prepare yourself

Before you attend the interview, there are several things that you can do (as well as reading this book) that will help you to prepare for the day. The trainee clinical psychologists surveyed spoke about the importance of familiarising yourself with undergraduate psychological theory, clinical examples, finding out about the course where you're interviewing and practicing interviews:

> 'Familiarise yourself with old notes from undergrad. You won't remember everything so pick out key theories and models that you feel apply to the courses that you are interviewing for.'

> 'You will feel much more confident drawing on lots of real examples when answering clinical questions.'

> 'Find out as much as you can about the interview for the course that you're interviewing for – all the courses are different.'

> 'Practice interview skills by taping yourself and watching back – I found this really helpful.'

> 'Do some mock interviews.'

'Practice the process of formulating an answer to questions, taking a deep breath structuring response, etc.'

'Think about current issues in the NHS, the pros and cons for different models and your own strengths and areas for development.'

'Don't prepare and revise so much that you end up burnt out in the interview.'

Be yourself

The trainee clinical psychologists spoke about the risk of becoming a 'generic responder' in interviews and how the interviewers want to get a sense of who *you* are. As a result, it's important not to be the 'perfect' candidate and to let your personality come through:

'Be yourself – not the person you think they want you to be.'

'Try to let your personality shine through.'

'Do not get too wedded or rehearsed in your answers – keep flexible and able to think on topic. You can think on the spot, you do it with service users all of the time.'

'Don't try to be the perfect candidate. Be aware of how you come across. Dress well.'

'Prepare enough so you feel competent but appear natural and non-robotic.'

Make the most of the opportunity

Similar to the previous themes, the interview is an opportunity for you to demonstrate who you are in relation to your skills, knowledge, passion and interests. The trainee clinical psychologists suggested that you should demonstrate how you can think flexibly, what you can add to the profession and what interests you have.

'Think about what your knowledge and experience have taught you and how you can personally add to the profession.'

'You are expected to demonstrate an ability to think, learn and utilise information to show that you will be able to make the most of the training.'

'Demonstrate an ability to think flexibly.'

'Have an interest; feminism, social constructionism, politics – something you can talk about that interests you and how that might impact the type of clinician you might be.'

'Be prepared to talk about your own "issues" for some courses – think about boundaries and the things that you would and would not feel comfortable sharing.'

'Remember that the interviewers don't know what a lovely and friendly person you are – you need to show them!'

Acknowledge your limits

The Doctorate in Clinical Psychology is a training program and thus, the interviewers don't expect you to be able to know everything. The trainee clinical psychologists suggested that you should not be afraid to pause and think after a question has been asked, and that you should acknowledge the things that you don't know and show your problem-solving skills.

'Know you limits and don't be afraid to voice them – be true to yourself and realistic in what you're trying to achieve.'

'Remember you're going to be training for three years so you're not expected to know everything now.'

'If you don't know say that you don't know. Then describe a way how you would work around the problem to understand more.'

'Pausing to answer question shows that your reflecting and considering your response. Ask the panel if you've answered the question.'

'They're not trying to trip you up – don't be afraid to speak about an idea even if you're unsure about it.'

'Be honest and say what you know rather than bluffing – they'll see right through it!'

Manage your anxiety

Interviews can be anxiety provoking and the trainee clinical psychologists suggested that you try to relax and not get caught up in the anxiety of the day by looking after yourself.

'I always do a Mindfulness-based relaxation exercise before interviews. Usually this involves mindful breathing to calm my anxiety.'

'I listen to a song that inspired me to help me.'

'Try to relax and not to panic.'

'Everyone has different strengths and weaknesses – focus on you and what you are bringing to the table.'

'Don't get caught up in the anxiety of the day. If you need to, take yourself out of the situation to a quiet room. There will be people asking you a million questions and bragging about the experience they have. They are probably just as nervous as you – try to ignore them.'

'Have a good sleep the day before, treat it like any other interview. Believe in yourself.'

Maintain perspective

Not being accepted on to a course following interview can be stressful and frustrating. However, the trainee clinical psychologists suggest that it is important to learn from these experiences, consider what other things you might want to do and not lose hope if you decide to apply again next year.

'Even if you don't get on you will learn something from the experience and it'll be worth it in the end.'

'If you don't have a successful interview think "I need to improve my experience or the way that I talk about my experience".'

'Think about other options and how you can fulfil your dreams in another way – this way you will be more likely to be yourself and less attached to the "outcome" of the interview.'

'There may be many random reasons why you don't get on to training in any individual year and it doesn't necessarily mean you never will.'

'The other people you are working with who have interviews are not the enemy.'

The trainee clinical psychology trainees had the following additional advice for anyone who is going through the process of application or interview.

'Live in the moment, focus less on the competition and pressures to get on.'

'Apply worry related therapy techniques to yourself – look at what you can influence and control rather than focusing on what you can't. Keep exercising and looking after yourself.'

'Try not to compare yourself to others, the competitiveness isn't always helpful and doesn't reflect your abilities as a psychologist.'

'Have as many interests and friends not related to training as possible.'

'Don't get sucked into comparing yourself to others who are applying to training. There will always be someone trying to show off and make you feel awful.'

'Be skilled at self-care – don't let clinical psychology be your entire life.'

'Talk to supportive others, have strategies to manage worry, do things that help you relax.'

'Accept that some stress is normal and be kind to yourself about that.'

SUMMARY

You should now be able to prepare for completing the application process and attending interviews for the Doctorate in Clinical Psychology. By answering the key question: 'Why do you want to be a clinical psychologist?' you'll be in a better position to answer the questions on the application form and in the interview. Applications are made through the Clearing House website and although the questions have remained similar over recent years, you should check the website for up to date application forms and submission dates. The trainee clinical psychologists stress the importance of putting in the ground work for the application and they suggested some ways to make your application stand out. They also said that it is important to manage your own expectations when completing the applications and ensuring that you maintain balance in your life.

Most people don't get invited to an interview after their first application for the Doctorate in Clinical Psychology so do not be disheartened if this happens. When you are invited to interview, there are four key areas that you should focus on: research, clinical work, current NHS issues and personal experiences. Most of the questions for the clinical training course will focus on one of these areas. The advice from trainee clinical psychologists in relation to interview was to ensure that you prepare and make the most of the opportunity. In the interview, they advised that you should be yourself and acknowledge your limits. As with the application process, the trainee clinical psychologists advised that you should consider how you can manage your anxiety and maintain perspective during the interview process.

Applying for clinical psychology training can be a long and frustrating process. There are a wide range of careers out there and it is important that you develop your skills as a person and don't become too focused on training as a clinical psychologist. In the next chapter of the book, we will help you to think about your strengths, skills and opportunities in order to consider if clinical psychology is the profession for you.

HOW DO I KNOW IF CLINICAL PSYCHOLOGY IS FOR ME?

Have you ever wondered or questioned whether clinical psychology is the right career path for you? If so, you're not alone. Many people who consider the profession contemplate this question at some point along the journey and even after qualifying! There are a variety of factors that will be considered in this chapter that will help you to work out how to choose the best path for you. It is useful throughout the processes considered in this book to continually ask yourself, 'do I really want to be a clinical psychologist?'

One of the common stumbling blocks that will be addressed in detail are unsuccessful applications to the course. As this chapter of the book progresses, we also highlight that receiving a 'rejection' can also give you a unique opportunity to take a step back to reflect and consider your values as well as possible alternative choices.

OUTCOMES FROM THE APPLICATION AND INTERVIEW PROCESS

Over the last seven years there have been between 3,528 and 3,932 applications for the Doctorate in Clinical Psychology across 30 universities in the UK each year. We have included Figure 6.1 here, again, to illustrate how many people applied per year, over the last seven years and how many of these were successful. Each year the success rate has been between 15 and 16% of all applications. This means that about 85% of applications are unsuccessful due to the high demand for places and limited availability. However, as noted in Chapter 5, your chances of

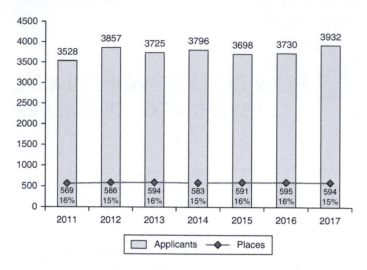

Figure 6.1 The number of applications made to clinical psychology training courses and the number of applicants accepted onto training from 2011 to 2017 (Clearing House, 2017).

being offered a place on training increase if you are invited for an interview.

What trainee clinical psychologists had to say!

The good news is that you are not alone in struggling with the application process. Both Steve and Amanda went through this process multiple times and the trainee clinical psychologists who we surveyed did too. Of the trainee clinical psychologists who completed the questionnaire, 12% had been successful after one application to training, 56% after two applications, 24% after three applications and 8% had applied four or more times before being accepted onto a course.

It is easy to feel discouraged when things don't go as planned, but this difficult experience can also provide an opportunity for self-reflection and creativity. It can allow you to continue to develop your professional skills, grow as a person and consider what might be right for you. There is no right way to manage a

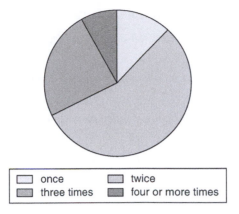

once   twice
three times   four or more times

Figure 6.2 The number of application attempts made to the clinical psychology training course by the trainee clinical psychologists who completed the survey.

disappointing outcome. The trainee clinical psychologists spoke about managing difficult emotions; seeking feedback, advice and support; improving professional skills; personal development and benefiting from hindsight.

Managing with difficult emotions

Several trainee clinical psychologists spoke about how the process of applying to be a clinical psychologist was emotionally challenging.

> *'I was very disheartened. I cried a lot over it and almost gave up trying.'*

> *'I was upset and disappointed but tried not to lose focus and determination.'*

> *'I allowed myself to experience the disappointment but then just got on with things.'*

> *'I felt defeated and upset. Then got over it by developing a plan of what I was going to do next and doing some things that I enjoy.'*

'There were definitely tears at first.'

'Disappointment and self-doubt, but also determination for the next round.'

'Sadness, dejection and anger, but also determination, focus and drive.'

'I picked myself back up (after moping for a few days) and focussed on being a stronger candidate the following year.'

'I was upset, but also a bit relieved as the location of the course was not ideal . . . I would have felt I had no choice had I been successful.'

'I was a bit grateful (in time) as I didn't particularly like the place I interviewed in and feel much happier where I am.'

Seeking feedback, advice and support

The trainee clinical psychologists spoke about the importance of accessing personal and professional support. They also spoke about how they were able to use feedback from the interview stage of the application in order to build on their experiences.

'I sought reassurance from my husband and family.'

'I sought feedback from the interview panel and discussed this with my supervisor who was able to support me.'

'I was a bit braver in seeking advice from colleagues the following year.'

'I was upset, but happy with the feedback I received. I worked hard to improve on the areas they had mentioned and applied again when I felt I met the criteria (which resulted in multiple offers of places).'

'Felt very miserable as many of my colleagues at the time were successful but I also used the feedback to change my strategy the following year. . .'

'I received some very helpful feedback . . . which I made a note of and felt confident it would help me next time.'

'Don't be too hard on yourself.'

'I remembered the numbers trying to get on this course.'

Improving professional skills

Some of the trainee clinical psychologists viewed the rejection from the course as an opportunity to consider how they could develop their skills ahead of the next round of applications.

'I took the failure to get a place as constructive criticism.'

'I decided to keep a reflective diary to help me think about how could improve my reflective skills which the panel said was a weakness.'

'After I regrouped I made a plan on how to give myself maximum chance of being successful next time. I applied learning points from the last interview.'

'I focussed on getting more experience.'

'I took the year to gain experience that I was lacking.'

'I got stuck into some other interesting work and study.'

'I spent the next year trying to think reflectively about my experiences in order to do a better application.'

'I lacked research experience, so I contacted my undergraduate Psychology Department and asked for an honorary position.'

'I had practice interviews. . . it was helpful to get feedback.'

'I used it as a learning experience and adapted my application.'

'I just viewed it as practice.'

Personal development

As well as developing their professional skills, some clinical psychologists used the experience of not being accepted onto a training course as an opportunity to understand themselves more and develop their skills in self-care.

> '*It made me think about how my self-worth was tied to my career and that I needed to spend more time developing my other interests and talents.*'

> '*I thought about why I wanted to get on training.*'

> '*I was determined not to let it rule my life.*'

> '*I made more effort to use self-care strategies.*'

> '*I invested in the book Mindset by Carol Dweck. This opened me up to a growth mindset . . . rather than a fixed mindset . . . it helped me to reframe the outcome and gave me the courage to reapply.*'

> '*I took a year off applying after I narrowly missed out . . . the year out helped me to reflect on whether this was right for me and I kept my mind open to other possibilities.*'

> '*I decided to explore other options so that I didn't have all my eggs in one basket, which reduced stress the next time.*'

> '*Used "plan b" and went travelling for a year and had a great time.*'

Benefiting from hindsight

The trainee clinical psychologists shared a sense that although rejection is hard to take at the time, distance brings perspective. When they look back on those times now, they realise that not getting on to the course at that point in their lives was the right outcome for them.

> '*I got four rejections the first year I applied . . . with hindsight, I was nowhere near ready.*'

> '*I wasn't too surprised . . . at that time, I applied without having any work experience.*'

'I tried to rationalise. . . I had just completed my undergraduate.'

'It turned out to be a blessing in disguise. At the time, I knew I wasn't quite ready. . .'

'In hindsight, it turned out to be the best thing that happened. The next assistant post I had was the most important clinical experience I had, and it really shaped how I wanted to practice as a clinical psychologist.'

'Four rejections one year do not mean it will be the same the next year.'

'I simply carried on through, confident that my application would be even stronger next year.'

'I said to myself, give it one more shot and I really went for it.'

As the extracts above have illustrated, there are a multitude of ways that trainees responded to an unsuccessful outcome. Here is a summary of the helpful ways to respond to enhance the chances of success later on:

- Making use of support systems, and actively seeking and making use of feedback in order to improve for the next time.
- Enhancing professional development through improving one's range of experiences and skill set.
- Thinking of the unsuccessful application and interview process as a learning experience.
- Actively pursuing personal growth after reflecting on the psychological impact of an unsuccessful outcome.
- Using hindsight to reflect on the benefits of not having obtained a place earlier on.
- Remaining hopeful for a successful future outcome despite what has occurred in the past.
- Taking a break from the application process and considering other interests and career options, which reduces stress and anxiety.
- Developing a compassionate and balanced way of looking at the outcome.

CONSIDERING YOUR VALUES IN CHOOSING TO PURSUE CLINICAL PSYCHOLOGY TRAINING

A combination of determination, resilience, maturity, self-awareness and self-reflection are important factors to help with future success. As mentioned above, some trainee clinical psychologists evaluated their reasons for wanting to train as a psychologist. It may be helpful for you to do the same.

As we considered in Chapters 3 to 5, it is important to reflect on the reason you want to become a clinical psychologist. It may be helpful to revisit this when considering if clinical psychology training is for you. What first attracted you to this work? It might be helpful to pin down memorable moments that made you curious and interested in becoming a clinical psychologist or supportive professional in Mental Health. Revisit the 'Have a go!' section from Chapter 5 and think about the reasons why you want to be a clinical psychologist.

Whatever the reasons may be, keep that with you as your big 'why' particularly during challenging times or when you are navigating through obstacles earlier or later down the line in your career journey. Your unique experiences along the career path will shape and mould your professional identity and how you feel about the career. Focussing on your values will also help you to maintain the ideals you hold for the kind of clinical psychologist you want to be.

What can I give and what will I gain?

When considering a career in a profession like clinical psychology it is important to consider what you feel you have to offer the people whom you work with. For instance, some people use their passion for social justice in the way that they practice and aim to reduce the impact of social inequalities in their work. Others have experienced a variety of supportive personal relationships and hope to create a similar safe and supportive space for many others who may have not had this. There are some who may use their lived experience of psychological distress to engage in their work as a clinical psychologist and support others. It is also important to think about what a career in clinical psychology can offer you too. Are the types of skills and knowledge accumulated by a clinical psychologist valuable to you? What would you consider to be stimulating and enriching opportunities that come with working as a clinical psychologist?

Who am I doing this for?

It can be tempting to begin and continue with a career for reasons that make it unsustainable and unfulfilling. It is important that you feel that you are pursuing the career because you want to and not because others expect you to. Sometimes expectations from family members, friends and colleagues can lead to people undertaking a career for less helpful reasons. In particular, when you are surrounded by other psychology students or assistant psychologists, competition can become the driving force. This can lead some people to pursue a career which they have some doubts or reservations about, without stopping to give themselves some space and to question the reasons why.

Are there things I haven't done that are important to me?

Completing the Doctorate in Clinical Psychology requires a commitment to an intellectually and emotionally demanding, full-time course that occupies most of your time during the three years of training. As a result, it is important to ensure that before you embark on the training course, you have had the opportunity to explore and do some things that you will have less time for during training.

What trainee clinical psychologists had to say!

Though several trainees we approached said that training came at the right time for them, a number of them gave examples of the things they would have liked to have pursued before obtaining a place on training. In particular, they spoke about how they would have liked more work and research experience, to pursue other interests and family goals before they began clinical psychology training.

Work and research experience

The trainee clinical psychologists spoke about how they would have wished to develop their research and clinical experiences in order to help them prepare for clinical psychology training.

> *'I would have liked to have a bit more research experience.'*

> *'I would have liked to strengthen my academic CV. Perhaps that would have made training less stressful for me.'*

> *'I wish I had done more research as I had minimal experience and now I am finding it difficult to do my thesis.'*

> *'Worked abroad a little.'*

> *'I wish I would have made the most of research opportunities and tried to publish my work.'*

> *'I could have done more clinical work, so that I felt more competent at this stage.'*

Other interests

Some people spoke about how prior to training they would have like to have travelled, worked abroad and spent more time doing their hobbies such as running.

> *'Travel more, up until I got onto the course, my life has been centred around getting valid experience and just getting into the course.'*

> *'Possibly running more marathons.'*

> *'Working abroad and travelling.'*

Family goals

Some of the trainee clinical psychologists spoke about how having children on the course could be challenging.

'It can be challenging to have a child whilst on the course.'

'I am sad that I do not have children at this point as three years is a long time to wait for this and I think it would be hard to juggle the demands of this role and parenting simultaneously.'

For most of the trainees who felt like the start of training came at the right time in their lives, they described having taken the time to do all the things they wanted prior to getting onto the course (e.g. one trainee wrote: *'I took ten years and did all those things [travelling, having children, doing more clinical and research work], in my 20s including working in psychology in other countries, pursuing other goals and in the process it has felt like there is little that I missed out on'*). Some trainees also acknowledged that they could do the things that they may have done after completing training (e.g. *'More travelling! But planning to go when I finish . . . only two years and eight months to go!'*).

Have a go!

Write down some responses to the following questions:

- How do you usually deal with rejection?
- What things can you put in place to manage this better?
- How might you develop personally and professionally over the next 12 months?
- What things would you like to do more of before you gain a place on clinical psychology training?

CONSIDERING OTHER OPTIONS

It can be helpful to think more broadly about what other career options you can consider. Some may be related to clinical psychology training and others will not be. Considering alternatives to clinical psychology training allows you to:

- Demonstrate your skills as a reflective individual who can consider multiple perspectives and choices, which is key to being an effective clinician, therapist or professional in any career or field;
- Evaluate what specific career path fits best with your values, personality, life goals and priorities;
- Broaden your choices;
- Reduce your anxiety by having a 'plan b';
- See how your degree and experience can be applied in different ways which is a reminder that you can change roles if you want to;
- Understand that a career choice can be revisited and re-evaluated throughout your life;
- Think about how your personal development and growth would progress based on the opportunities afforded by each path (e.g. psychotherapists and counselling psychologists are required to have their own personal therapy).

CAREERS RELATED TO CLINICAL PSYCHOLOGY

This section will consider career paths in Healthcare which are related or affiliated with skills that a clinical psychologist uses in their work. Many people that study psychology (or other social sciences) and take up positions within Mental Health, Physical Health, Forensic and Educational settings will have gained a varied and valuable skill set that are important in many different careers. Many of these alternatives can be overlooked, particularly for those who study psychology at A-level and undergraduate degree level. Some examples include CBT therapist, educational psychologist, counselling psychologist, mental health social worker, systemic family therapist, occupational therapist, mental health nurse and psychiatrist.

Examples of alternatives

CBT therapist

What do they do? Support people to reduce emotional distress by helping them to make changes in their thought and behaviour patterns.

Qualifications required to undertake training. Usually an undergraduate degree or professional qualification, including social work, nursing, psychologist, counsellor, teacher, pastoral worker, music, drama or art therapist.

Experience and skills required. Voluntary or paid experience in Mental Health Care or service offering psychotherapy.

Years training and qualification. A minimum of one year's full time Postgraduate Diploma in Cognitive Behaviour Therapy (CBT). Some courses are longer and offered on a part-time basis.

How much do they earn? Starting salary can be approximately £25,000 depending on your location and area of work.

Educational psychologist

What do they do? Support people in Educational settings who have learning difficulties, emotional, social and developmental problems.

Qualifications required to undertake training. An accredited psychology degree or conversion course.

Experience and skills required. Experience in Educational settings, e.g. learning support assistant or speech and language therapist in a school,

Years training and qualification. Three-year Doctorate in Educational Psychology, in England.

How much do they earn? Starting salary approximately £35,000 depending on your location and area of work.

Counselling psychologist

What do they do? Support people who are distressed and work with issues such as bereavement, trauma and relationship issues. Self-awareness and interpersonal dynamics are central to this work.

Qualifications required to undertake training. An accredited psychology undergraduate degree or conversion course.

Experience and skills required. Experience in Mental Health settings, e.g. psychological wellbeing practitioner or support worker.

Years training and qualification. A three-year Doctorate in Counselling Psychology, in England.

How much do they earn? Starting salary approximately £31,000 depending on your location and area of work.

Social worker in mental health

What do they do? Provide support and empowerment to individuals who have experienced mental health difficulties to help them lead fulfilling lives. The work can also involve the person's family, carers and their community.

Qualifications required to undertake training. At least three A-levels, along with 5 GCSEs A*–C, including English and maths.

Experience and skills required. Experience in Mental Health or Physical Health Care settings; voluntary work and personal experience is also accepted as valuable. Peer support workers are required to identify as having a living experience of mental health problems.

Years training and qualification. Approximately three years of degree-level training, if you have a degree in another subject you can study a diploma or Master's Degree (MA/MSc) in Social Work between one to two years.

How much do they earn? Starting salary can be approximately £21,000–£26,000 depending on your location and area of work.

Systemic family therapist

What do they do? Seek to reduce distress by improving the systems of interaction between people in relationships such as families, couples, carer-service user relationships.

Some systemic practitioners also work with wider systems such as staff teams, organisations and governments.

Qualifications required to undertake training. Usually an undergraduate degree or professional qualification, including social work, nursing, psychologist, counsellor, teacher, pastoral worker, music, drama or art therapist.

Experience and skills required. Clinical experience in the above or similar professions and working with families or relational issues can help.

Years training and qualification. Often can be a two-year, part-time, Master's Degree (MA/MSc) in Systemic Psychotherapy or Family Therapy.

How much do they earn? Starting salary approximately £25,000–£38,000 depending on your location and area of work.

Psychodynamic psychotherapist

What do they do? Help people to understand and resolve psychological distress or relational problems. This is achieved through improving awareness of the impact of someone's 'unconscious' and internal world, including early childhood experiences.

Qualifications required to undertake training. Undergraduate degree or postgraduate qualifications, e.g. a Postgraduate Diploma in Psychotherapeutic Counselling.

Experience and skills required. Work experience with a relevant clinical population in Mental Health or Social Care settings.

Years training and qualification. Often two to three-year, part-time, Master's Degree in Psychodynamic Psychotherapy depending on the type of course, previous qualifications and experience.

How much do they earn? Average salary can be about £34,000 depending on your location and area of work.

Occupational therapist

What do they do? Work with people with a range of mental, neurological and physical difficulties to improve their ability to perform day to day tasks and engage in meaningful activities.

Qualifications required to undertake training. Usually a minimum of two A-levels are needed in addition to 5 GCSE's at grade A*–C.

Experience and skills required. If you already have a relevant postgraduate degree and Healthcare experience, you can apply for a undergraduate Diploma or Master's Degree in Occupational Therapy.

Years training and qualification. A three to four-year undergraduate degree in occupational therapy or Master's level qualification, which takes two years.

How much do they earn? Starting salary approximately £21,000–£27,000 depending on your location and area of work.

Mental health nurse

What do they do? Provide support and nursing care to people who have a mental health problem and people experiencing acute psychological distress.

Qualifications required to undertake training. A-levels.

Experience and skills required. Experience in Mental Health or Physical Health Care settings

Years training and qualification. Three-year study for an undergraduate degree in mental health nursing.

How much do they earn? Starting salary can be approximately £23,000 depending on your location and area of work.

Psychiatrist

What do they do? Provide 'diagnosis' and 'treatment' for people assessed to have a mental health problem as defined by diagnostic manuals such as the *International Classification of Diseases* (ICD) and the *Diagnostic and Statistical Manual of Mental Disorders* (DSM). Psychiatrists can sometimes also provide psychological support for people and some train as psychotherapists as well.

Qualifications required to undertake training. Undergraduate degree in medicine.

Experience and skills required. Experience in Mental Health Care settings as part of specialist training in psychiatry.

Years training and qualification. Approximately eight years of paid postgraduate training in psychiatry.

How much do they earn? Speciality doctors in psychiatry can earn approximately £37,000–£100,000+ depending on your location and area of work.

There is not scope to cover all potential, related career paths in this book. Therefore, a number of career options were not considered above. These include:

- behavioural analyst;
- cognitive analytic therapist;
- forensic psychologist;
- occupational or business psychologist;
- postgraduate clinical researcher;
- lecturer and researcher;
- art/drama therapist.

These careers are also related to clinical psychology training and will require some of the same skills and further information regarding these career paths can be found online. If you decide to research these roles, it is important to discover more about what the course/educational requirements will demand from you, what you will learn, what will be added to your existing skill set and if the career option fits with your values and financial aims.

What trainee clinical psychologists had to say!

The trainees we approached gave some examples of roles, related to clinical psychology, which they may have considered if they did not get a place on clinical training. Several respondents said that they have never considered another career option.

Alternatives considered

'Medicine, then go down the neurology, neuropsychiatry or psychiatry route.'

'Something medical.'

'I think if I didn't get a place on training and I'd gotten the experience in Mental Health settings, I would have retrained as an occupational therapist.'

'Research in psychology.'

'Family therapy would have been the most likely option.'

'Social work or counselling.'

'Psychotherapy or teaching.'

'Counselling psychologist.'

'Perhaps a teacher or therapist of some kind.'

'I would have trained as a CBT therapist.'

'I had thought about training as a registered mental health nurse if I did not get on.'

'I would have run or set up a mental health charity.'

> **Have a go!**
>
> Write down your responses to the following questions:
>
> - What careers would interest me that are similar to clinical psychology?
> - What is it about these roles that I would enjoy?
> - What would my 'plan b' look like if I was to work in a similar profession?

CAREERS UNRELATED TO CLINICAL PSYCHOLOGY: WHERE ELSE CAN I APPLY MY INTERESTS, EXPERIENCE AND SKILLS?

If you have been following a path to a career in clinical psychology, it is important to remember that the skills you have built are both valuable and transferrable. As a result, you will be able to use these to ensure that your application stands out in relation to a range of careers. These transferrable skills include:

- Communication skills, which help resolve conflicts, diffuse situations or enhance the experience of a service. Clear, consistent communication is important in any role seeking user/client perspectives or experiences.
- Interpersonal skills such as empathy, which allow you to communicate information in a sensitive way that meets the needs of the individual.
- Therapy skills helpful in understanding and motivating others, exploring barriers in development and performance, formulating difficulties and being able to effectively support the development of others within a team or business.
- Improved self-awareness and flexibility in your approach to work.
- Understanding psychological theories and concepts about how people learn and develop, how they change, how they develop relationships and community with others and the multifaceted factors that lead to a breakdown in productivity and motivation.
- The ability to analyse and critique data which helps with most organisations that want to measure their performance.

What trainee clinical psychologists had to say!

When asked what careers outside of clinical psychology they have considered, the trainee clinical psychologists spoke about the following diverse range of careers. This list of different careers demonstrates that there is a wide range of career paths and roles that trainees would have been open to considering had they not been pursuing clinical psychology. The trainees had a rich range of ideas for their careers.

'Medicine, fashion, fashion photography, writing.'

'Sports or performance psychology.'

'Teaching maths and history.'

'Possibly a teacher or maybe mental health nursing.'

'Running a business and helping people to be the best they can be.'

'I love writing and would have liked (in another life) to be a journalist.'

'Probably a career in music, teaching and performing.'

'Before starting university, I had an interest in chemistry.'

'Probation officer.'

'Possibly counselling or party planning!'

'Service design – combining psychology and design principles to work as part of a Design Team, aimed at creating better services for Health and Social Care.'

'International development.'

'Social anthropology, commissioning or public health.'

'Art, design, sports or maybe medicine?'

'I would have pursued one of my other strong passions – art.'

'Maybe architecture.'

'Family business – property management and development.'

'Lifestyle entrepreneur or author.'

Have a go!

Write down your response to the following questions:

- What interests do you have? They can be related to anything!
- When you were younger, what things did you want to do, when you 'grew up'?
- What skills do you have that could be applied to other careers?
- If clinical psychology didn't exist what would you do?

SUMMARY

We hope that this chapter helped you to learn more about how common it is to get an undesirable outcome after applying to the clinical psychology course, but that it is possible to recover from that disappointment. As demonstrated by the trainees who experienced this, an unsuccessful outcome can help you to grow and develop further. By learning from the experience, as difficult as it may feel at first, you stand to become a more skilled, experienced and resilient clinician by the time you begin your training. This chapter also explored how important it is not to 'place all your eggs in one basket' and to consider your values and reasons for applying specifically for clinical psychology training. It is important to consider a variety of career options. By doing this, you can reduce stress and anxiety because you have a variety of options. If something doesn't work out, you can learn from the experience and creatively consider other ways forward.

Clinical psychology is not for everyone; you should feel free to change your mind or take a break from the career path without the sense of pressure to keep pursuing it. Don't forget that the skills and knowledge that you already possess are highly valuable and essential across many fields within and outside of psychology. Also remember that your career journey is distinctive from anyone else's, despite apparent similarities with your peers. Your unique career journey, with all its ups and downs, is part of what shapes you as a person and professional, so learn all that you can from it.

Whether you come with a different career background, have more years between your degree and starting the course, or have a different educational path, those experiences matter. Having applied one or five times, being from an ethnic minority background, having your own experiences of mental health problems, having a disability or having children should not be a barrier should you wish to pursue clinical psychology. These experiences shape your journey. Instead of comparing yourself to your peers' circumstances and their apparent achievements, you stand to gain much more through appreciating the development of your own unique story of joining the career. Adopting this approach to your career helps with developing self-reflection and self-awareness. It also helps with valuing your own difference and diversity as an asset rather than viewing it as a barrier. When you value your own journey, your confidence in your place within the profession is more likely to be better established.

CONCLUSION

Clinical psychology is a unique, interesting and challenging career and clinical psychologists are fortunate to work in a wide range of interesting ways across a range of settings. One of the greatest barriers to understanding if clinical psychology is for you is making sense of the acronyms, ideas, theories and similar careers. This book is designed to make this process easier for you and we hope that it has been helpful to you in considering becoming a clinical psychologist in the UK.

Throughout the book we have included a wide range of resources including academic references, personal experiences and survey data from 70 clinical psychologists representing 12 of the UK's clinical psychology training courses. We also presented the responses of professionals training and working in clinical psychology. These responses included six detailed profiles provided by trainee clinical psychologists and six provided by qualified clinical psychologists. The survey data and the profiles will have provided you with a varied insight into what it is like to train as a clinical psychologist and what it can be like to work as a clinical psychologist in a wide range of services. The people who completed the profiles represent a diverse and varied group of trainee and qualified clinical psychologists and although there were several differences in their pre-training experience, their advice to anyone applying to clinical psychology training was very similar and focused on the key messages:

- Maintain balance throughout your career journey and develop your other interests. Remember that your life should always be about more than applying to train as a clinical psychologist.
- Make the most of any professional opportunities that arise throughout your undergraduate degree and once you begin to gain work experience.

- Use any experiences you have as an opportunity to reflect, learn and develop as a person and psychologist.
- Consider what will make you a good clinical psychologist and show who you are whenever possible.
- There is no rush to get onto training, remain persistent and tenacious.

In Chapter 4, about making the most of your experience, we described some of the ways that aspiring clinical psychologists can begin to develop the skills that they require to enable them to be successful in their career. Commonly people will undertake roles that focus on research and/or clinical work. These roles can include working as a research assistant, support worker, volunteer, assistant psychologists and psychological wellbeing practitioner. Alongside increasing your experience in these areas, it is important to consider opportunities for learning and skill development, often referred to as continued professional development or CPD. You should also make the most of opportunities to develop professional networks which may lead to further opportunities.

In Chapter 5 we considered the importance of preparation for applications and interviews, providing a summary of useful information for people applying for the doctorate in clinical psychology. First of all, it is important to know why you want to be a clinical psychologist as this has to be clearly communicated through your application form. At the interview stage, there are several approaches, such as the STARR (Situation, Target, Action, Result and Reflection) model that you can apply to questions relating to research, clinical work, current NHS and professional issues and personal experiences. To maximise your performance throughout this process, you should aim to maintain balance and perspective, manage your expectations and anxiety whilst making the most of the opportunity.

The final section of the book provided an overview of the alternative careers that you may undertake that are similar to clinical psychology and those that are different. We encourage you to think about how you might want to apply your skills in other ways. There are a wide range of career options that are related to clinical psychology and even more that are not. Considering what else you might want to do will help you to pursue a career that fits with your values and how you want to work, whilst bearing in mind how this can change over time. Above all, your journey to clinical psychology training or whatever career you choose will be one of continuous learning!

We hope that whatever career you decide to pursue in the future, clinical psychology or otherwise, it fits with your values, gives you a sense of purpose and enables you to feel useful. Good luck!

APPENDIX

Summary of charities for volunteer opportunities

ACTION ON ADDICTION – www.actiononaddiction.org.uk

Action on Addiction is a UK-based charity that provides support for individuals affected by a drug and/or alcohol addiction. The service works in the areas of research in the area of addiction, provides treatment and aftercare support. In addition, this charity provides professional education and support for families and carers of people affected by addiction.

ADDACTION – www.addaction.org.uk

Addaction is a charity based in the UK that supports individuals with their drug and alcohol use as well as any mental health difficulties they might be facing. Addaction aims to help people change their behaviour in order to make lasting positive changes to their lives.

BEAT – www.beateatingdisorders.org.uk

Beat is a charity that supports individuals affected by emotional difficulties associated with eating. A number of people accessing support from this charity may have a formal diagnosis of an eating 'disorder'. The charity provides advice, information and support via helplines as well as local and online support groups.

HEADWAY – www.headway.org.uk

Headway is a UK-wide charity that aims to improve the lives of people that have been affected by a brain injury. Headway provides support, Clinical Services and information to survivors of brain injury and their carers, families as well as professionals working in health and the legal sectors.

MIND – www.mind.org.uk

Mind is a mental health charity that operates within England and Wales offering advice and support to individuals with a mental health difficulty. Mind also campaigns to raise awareness, promote better understanding, empower people and improve Mental Health Service provision.

RETHINK – www.rethink.org

Rethink are a mental health charity that provides expert advice and information to anyone affected by mental health difficulties. Rethink also run multiple Mental Health Services and support groups across England. These include Psychological Therapy Services, crisis and recovery homes, housing support and peer support groups. Rethink are also involved in campaigning for national policy change that aims to improve the lives of people affected by mental health problems.

SAMARITANS – www.samaritans.org

Samaritans is a charity accessible throughout UK and Ireland that offers a 24-hour confidential telephone service to anyone who requires emotional support. Samaritans workers support those in any kind of emotional distress, including people who are struggling to cope with the demands of life or people who are at risk of suicide.

SANE – www.sane.org.uk

Sane is a charity that operates in the UK and works to improve the quality of life of people with mental health difficulties. The charity's aims include reducing stigma about having mental health problems, raising awareness through campaigns to improve services and research to improve mental health outcomes. This charity also provides emotional support for people with mental health problems, their families and carers as well as providing information for organisations and the wider public.

TOGETHER – www.together-uk.org

Together is a UK-based charity that provides a wide range of support services to help manage the personal and practical impact of living with mental health difficulties. The services include supported accommodation as well as one-to-one support in the community.

REFERENCES

APA (2017). 'Clinical psychology' definition. Retrieved from: www.apa.org/ed/graduate/specialize/clinical.aspx.

Bentall, P. (2003). *Madness Explained: Psychosis and Human Nature*. Penguin Books, London.

Clearing House (2017). Numbers and graduate employment. Retrieved from: www.leeds.ac.uk/chpccp/numbers.html.

Farndon, H. (2016). HCPC registered psychologists in the UK. British Psychological Society. Retrieved from: http://beta.bps.org.uk/sites/beta.bps.org.uk/files/Policy%20-%20Files/HCPC%20Registered%20Psychologists%20in%20the%20UK.pdf.

General Medical Council (2017). List of registered medical practitioners – statistics. Retrieved from: www.gmc-uk.org/doctors/register/search_stats.asp.

Georgiadis, N. & Phillmore, L. (1985). The myth of the hero innovator and alternative strategies for organizational change. In *Behaviour Modification with the Severely Retarded*. I. Hanley & J. Hodge (eds.). Associated Scientific Publishers, New York.

Gibbs, G. (1988). *Learning by Doing: A Guide to Teaching and Learning Methods*. Further Education Unit. Oxford Polytechnic, Oxford.

Hall, J., Pilgrim, D. & Turpin, G. (eds.). (2015). *Clinical Psychologists in Britain: Historical Perspectives*. British Psychological Society, London.

Hannigan, B., Edwards, D. & Burnard, P. (2004). Stress and stress management in clinical psychology: findings from a systematic review. *Journal of Mental Health*, *13*(3): 235–245.

Johns, C. (1995). Framing learning through reflection within Carper's fundamental ways of knowing in nursing. *Journal of Advanced Nursing, 22*(2): 226–234.

Johnstone, L. (2000). *Users and Abusers of Psychiatry: A Critical Look at Psychiatric Practice*. Routledge, London.

Johnstone, L. & Boyle, M. with Cromby, J., Dillon, J., Harper, D., Kinderman, P., Longden, E., Pilgrim, D. & Read, J. (2018). *The Power Threat Meaning Framework: Overview*. British Psychological Society, Leicester.

Johnstone, L. & Dallas, R. (2014). *Formulation in Psychology and Psychotherapy: Making Sense of People's Problems*. Routledge (2nd Edition), East Sussex.

Llewelyn, S. & Murphy, D. J. (eds.) (2014). *What is Clinical Psychology?* Oxford University Press (5th Edition), Oxford.

McGrath, L., Walker, C. & Jones, C. (2016). Psychologists against austerity: mobilising psychology for social change. *Critical and Radical Social Work, 4*(3): 409–413.

The Mental Health Taskforce (2016). *The Five Year Forward View for Mental Health*. National Health Service, England.

Strupp, H. H. & Anderson, T. (1997). On the limitations of therapy manuals. *Clinical Psychology: Science and Practice, 4*(1): 76–82.

INDEX

A-levels 65–66, 92, 122, 124, 126
academic work 65–68, 89;
    see also degrees
Action on Addiction 136
Addaction 136
addiction 2, 136
administrative work 76, 80
Adult Learning Disabilities
    57–58
Adult Mental Health 34, 49–50, 61
advice, seeking 88, 114–115
American Psychological
    Association (APA) 93
anxiety 2, 4, 44, 78, 131; job
    interviews 86; 'plan b' 122;
    preparation for training
    interviews 107, 109, 134
application process 17–20,
    90–110, 134; application form
    77, 92–97, 109; dealing with
    rejection 97–98, 107–108,
    112–117, 131; improving
    your job applications 84–85;
    interviews 97–109; number of
    applicants 18–19, 111–112;
    qualified psychologists'
    experiences 44, 47, 54, 58;
    trainees' experiences 28,
    30–31, 34, 37–38
Assertive Outreach (AO) Service
    50–51
assessment 2, 3, 57, 68, 75–76
assistant psychologists 68, 69,
    75–77, 88; competitiveness
    for posts 56, 58, 76; honorary
    31–32, 72; networking 84

Association for Clinical
    Psychologists (ACP-UK) xi
austerity 11, 20, 102
autonomy 53, 58

balance 60, 63, 96–97,
    133, 134
Beat 136
boundaries 72
brain assessments 3, 75–76
British Psychological Society
    (BPS) xi, 16, 66, 75, 77, 84
Brown, Derren 9
budget cuts 11, 20
burn-out 20

CBT *see* Cognitive Behavioural
    Therapy
charities 70–72, 81, 136–138
Child and Adolescent Mental
    Health Services 22–23, 30, 37
children: assessment of 3;
    Paediatric Health Psychology
    46–47
Clearing House for Postgraduate
    Courses in Clinical Psychology
    x–xi, 16, 17–18, 92, 109
clinical experience 68–69,
    88–89; application form
    93; assistant psychologists
    75; CBT therapists 123;
    counselling psychologists
    124; educational psychologists
    123; job applications 85;
    mental health nurses 126;
    occupational therapists 126;

preparation for interviews
100–101, 109; psychiatrists
127; psychodynamic
psychotherapists 125;
psychological wellbeing
practitioners 78; requirements
for doctoral course 16–17,
21; research assistants 79–80;
social workers in mental
health 124; specific roles
70–83, 134; systemic family
therapists 125; trainees'
experiences 33, 38–39, 41,
120; wide range of 87
clinical psychology: alternative
careers to 121–129, 134–135;
careers unrelated to 129–131;
choosing to pursue training
118–121; clients 1–2; current
challenges 10–11, 63;
definition of 1; key messages
133–134; myths about
clinical psychologists 7–10,
21; negative aspects 20–21;
reasons for becoming a clinical
psychologist 11–16, 21, 23–24,
26, 28–29, 31–32, 35–36,
38–39, 44–45, 48, 51, 55,
58–59, 62, 90–91; trainees'
experiences 22–42; training
requirements 16–20, 21; ways
of working 2–7; working as a
clinical psychologist 43–64
Clinical Psychology Forum 76, 102
Clinical Services 14
ClinPsyD *see* Doctorate in
Clinical Psychology
'co-production' of services 6
Cognitive Behavioural Therapy
(CBT) 11, 37, 67, 78, 122–123
collaboration 9
communication 5, 67–68, 129
Community Mental Health
Teams (CMHTs) 50
Community Psychology 6–7, 51

competitiveness 17, 18–19, 20,
21, 119; assistant psychologist
posts 56, 58, 76; trainee advice
108
conferences 67–68, 84, 87
confidence 48–49, 61, 66, 87
consultation 5
continual professional
development (CPD) 83,
93, 134
conversion courses 66, 93,
123, 124
counselling psychologists
123–124
CPD *see* continual professional
development
critical thinking 88
cultural issues 26–27, 38
curiosity 12, 29, 38, 49, 59

DClinPsy *see* Doctorate in
Clinical Psychology
DCP *see* Division of Clinical
Psychology
degrees 66–68, 89, 122, 133;
assistant psychologists
75; CBT therapists 123;
counselling psychologists
124; educational psychologists
123; psychiatrists
127; psychodynamic
psychotherapists 125;
psychological wellbeing
practitioners 77; requirements
for doctoral course 16, 93;
research assistants 79; systemic
family therapists 125
depression 2, 78
diversity 42, 64, 132; qualified
psychologists' experiences 45,
48–49, 51–52, 55–56, 59, 62,
63; trainees' experiences 24,
26–27, 29, 32, 36, 39–40, 41
Division of Clinical Psychology
(DCP) xi, 76, 84, 102

Doctorate in Clinical Psychology (DClinPsy/DClinPsych/ClinPsyD) x, 16, 17–20, 33; clinical experience 68; demanding nature of course 119; number of applicants 18–19, 111–112; preparing for applications and interviews 90–110; research 7; *see also* application process; training
Dweck, Carol 116

educational psychologists 123
emotional challenges: dealing with rejection 113–114; support work 74; training 20, 34–35, 37; volunteer work 72
empathy 129
ethnicity 29, 32, 45, 52, 59, 132
evaluation 2, 4–5, 68–69
evidence 10, 14, 80
expectations 84, 96, 109, 119, 134

family issues 120–121
family therapy 57, 124–125
feedback 86, 88, 114–115, 117
Five Year Forward View 102
Forensic Services 43–44, 45, 122
formulation 2, 3–4, 5, 37, 68, 78
Freud, Sigmund 8–9
funding cuts 11, 20

gender 45
Graduate Basis for Chartered Membership (GBC) 66

Headway 136–137
Health and Care Professions Council (HCPC) xi, 10
healthcare assistants 73–75, 88–89
helping others 15, 58
helpline work 69, 70–71
hindsight 116–117

honorary assistant psychologists 31–32, 72
hospitals 1–2, 46–47, 53, 72

IAPT *see* Improving Access to Psychological Therapies
identity 41, 51, 87, 118
imagery work 30
imposter syndrome 55
Improving Access to Psychological Therapies (IAPT) 35, 78, 79, 89
Intensive Short-Term Dynamic Psychotherapy (ISTDP) 61
interventions 2, 4, 68
interviews: advice from trainees 104–109; applying for a doctorate course 18, 77, 97–109, 134; assessment 3; feedback 114; improving your interview skills 86; qualified psychologists' experiences 54, 58; research assistants 80; trainees' experiences 23, 31, 34, 37–38

job requirements 85

knowing your limits 106–107

leadership 6, 66, 68–69
learning 63, 83, 89
learning disabilities 57–58

MDTs *see* Multi-Disciplinary Teams
media 102
medical model 10–11
mental health 13, 38, 62; charities 137–138; personal experiences 132; psychological wellbeing practitioners 77–79; social workers 124; volunteer work 70–72
mental health nurses 126

Mental Health Services 8, 34, 49–50, 61, 102, 122; CBT therapists 123; charities 137; counselling psychologists 124; impact of austerity on 11; mental health nurses 126; power dynamics 45

Mind 137

Multi-Disciplinary Teams (MDTs) 25, 36, 44, 53, 57–58, 69, 76

myths 7–10, 21

National Health Service (NHS) 1, 19, 63, 87; assistant psychologists 68, 77; bureaucracy 61; knowledge of key issues in the 96, 98, 102, 105, 109; pay scales 84; pressures 35–36; psychological wellbeing practitioners 78, 79; research assistants 81; support work 74

networking 84, 134

neuropsychological assessments 3, 75–76

neuropsychological rehabilitation 53

NHS *see* National Health Service

occupational therapists 126

older adults 28

Oncology 25

Paediatric Health Psychology 46–47

Palliative Care 25

pay scales 19, 44, 84; *see also* salaries

personal development 26, 37, 71, 116, 117, 122

personal experiences 13, 16, 91, 118, 132; preparation for interviews 102–103, 109;

qualified psychologists' experiences 44–45, 51, 58

personality disorders 34

placements: diversity 26; qualified psychologists' experiences 47, 51–52; trainees' experiences 23, 25, 28, 31–32, 34, 37; during undergraduate degree 67; *see also* work experience

'plan b' 116, 122, 129

post-traumatic stress 2

Power Threat Meaning Framework (PTMF) 102

pre-interview assessments 97

preparation 87, 94–95, 98–103, 104–105, 109, 134

proactivity 81, 88

professional development 2, 26, 37, 68–69, 83, 93, 117, 134

psychiatrists 8, 127

psychoanalysis 8–9

psychodynamic psychotherapists 125

psychological wellbeing practitioners (PWPs) 69, 77–79

Psychologist magazine 77

Psychologists for Social Change (PSC) xi–xii, 7

Psychology A-level 65–66, 122

Psychology degrees 16, 66–68, 75, 77, 93, 122; *see also* degrees

psychosis 2

publications 67–68, 80, 89, 93

PWPs *see* psychological wellbeing practitioners

qualifications 65–68; applying for a doctorate course 92–93; assistant psychologists 75; CBT therapists 123; counselling psychologists 124; educational psychologists 123; mental health

nurses 126; occupational therapists 126; psychiatrists 127; psychodynamic psychotherapists 125; psychological wellbeing practitioners 77; research assistants 79; social workers in mental health 124; systemic family therapists 125; *see also* degrees
questionnaires 3, 4, 71, 75, 80

references 94
reflection 37, 41, 88, 134; application form 95; preparation for interviews 98; psychological wellbeing practitioners 78; STARR approach 99
reflective diaries/journals 79, 82
reflective practitioners 2
reflexivity 56
Rehabilitation and Recovery Services 23, 30, 53–54
rejections 97–98, 107–108, 109, 111, 112–117, 131
relationships 6, 21, 51; networking 84; research assistants 81; support work 73
religion 39–40, 59, 62
research 7, 14, 68–69; assistant psychologists 76; preparation for interviews 99–100, 109; trainees' experiences 120
research assistants 58, 69, 72, 79–81
resilience 41, 58–59, 88–89, 118
Rethink 137
risk management 34, 44

safety 72, 73
salaries: assistant psychologists 75; CBT therapists 123; counselling psychologists 124; educational psychologists

123; expectations 84; mental health nurses 126; occupational therapists 126; psychiatrists 127; psychodynamic psychotherapists 125; psychological wellbeing practitioners 78; research assistants 79; social workers in mental health 124; support workers 73; systemic family therapists 125; trainees 19
Samaritans 137
Sane 137
scientist practitioners 2, 10
Secondary Care Adult Mental Health Service 34
self-awareness 32, 118, 123, 129, 132
self-care 63, 88, 109, 116
self-management 10–11
service development 6
sexuality 32
shadowing 71, 76–77, 81
shift work 74
skills 35–36, 110; alternative careers 122; assistant psychologists 75, 76; CBT therapists 123; communication 5, 67–68, 129; continual professional development 83; counselling psychologists 124; educational psychologists 123; improving your professional skills 69, 112, 115, 117; job interviews 86; mental health nurses 126; occupational therapists 126; psychiatrists 127; psychodynamic psychotherapists 125; psychological wellbeing practitioners 78, 79; research assistants 79; social workers in mental health 124; support work 73; systemic family therapists 125; transferable 23,

129, 131–132; volunteer work 70–71
social change 6
social media 102
social workers 124
STARR approach 99, 134
stigma 38, 40, 137
stress 63, 72, 76, 109, 116, 131
supervision 2, 5, 37, 68–69, 87; assistant psychologists 75, 77; psychological wellbeing practitioners 78–79; qualified psychologists' experiences 54, 58; research assistants 81
support work 69, 73–75, 77
systemic family therapists 124–125
systemic work 6–7

teaching 5, 68–69
therapeutic interventions 2, 4
therapy skills 129
time management 36
Together 138
training 8, 11, 16–20, 21, 134; assistant psychologists 77; CBT therapists 123; choosing to pursue 118–121; counselling psychologists 124; dealing with rejection 97–98, 107–108, 112–117, 131; educational psychologists 123; mental health nurses 126; occupational therapists 126; preparing for applications and interviews 90–110, 134; psychiatrists 127; psychodynamic psychotherapists 125; psychological wellbeing practitioners 78; social workers in mental health 124; support workers 73; systemic family

therapists 125; trainees' experiences 22–42, 119–121; volunteer work 70–71; see also application process; Doctorate in Clinical Psychology
transferable skills 23, 129, 131–132
trauma 30, 38–39, 118

undergraduate degrees 66–68, 89, 122, 133; assistant psychologists 75; CBT therapists 123; counselling psychologists 124; educational psychologists 123; psychiatrists 127; psychodynamic psychotherapists 125; psychological wellbeing practitioners 77; requirements for doctoral course 16, 93; research assistants 79; systemic family therapists 125
University of Hull 17
University of York 17

volunteering 66, 67, 68, 69, 70–72

Widening Access to Clinical Psychology Scheme 39, 40
wider systemic work 6–7
work experience 41, 68–69, 133; application form 93; specific roles 70–83; trainees' experiences 120; during undergraduate degree 67; wide range of 87; see also clinical experience; placements
working hours 73–74
workload 47; psychological wellbeing practitioners 78, 79; research assistants 81